THE BOOK OF
CHOCOLATE

THE AMAZING STORY OF THE WORLD'S FAVORITE CANDY

HP Newquist

VIKING

ONE *of the only things on Earth sweeter than chocolate is music.*
This book is dedicated to every musician who has inspired me,
and every musician I've had the privilege of performing with.

VIKING

An imprint of Penguin Random House LLC

375 Hudson Street

New York, New York 10014

First published in the United States of America by Viking, an imprint of Penguin Random House LLC, 2017

Copyright © 2017 by HP Newquist

LIBRARY OF CONGRESS CATALOGING-IN-PUBLICATION DATA

Newquist, H. P. (Harvey P.), author.

The book of chocolate : the amazing story of the world's favorite candy / HP Newquist.—First American edition.

pages cm

Includes bibliographical references and index.

ISBN 978-0-670-01574-0 (hardcover) 1. Chocolate industry—Juvenile literature. 2. Chocolate industry—History—Juvenile
literature. 3. Chocolate—Juvenile literature. 4. Chocolate—History—Juvenile literature. I. Title.

HD9200.A2N49 2016   338.4'76639209—dc23   2015031930

Manufactured in China

Designed by Nancy Brennan

Set in Sentinel

1   3   5   7   9   10   8   6   4   2

CONTENTS

◆◆◆◆◆◆◆◆◆◆◆◆◆◆◆◆◆◆◆◆◆

INTRODUCTION

CHOCOLATE. THERE'S NOTHING ELSE LIKE IT ON THE PLANET. Just saying the word *chocolate* evokes thoughts of deliciousness, sweetness, and irresistibility.

Pick a flavor. Pick a sweet. Pick your favorite thing to eat. For nearly everyone who reads this book, chocolate is going to be their favorite flavor, or in their top two or three.

There is something special about chocolate. The way it tastes, the way it looks, smells, and feels. The way it is packaged and wrapped. The way it is given as a gift, as a treat, as a reward. No other food has the power to evoke emotions the way chocolate does. If you don't think so, try giving someone chicken as a gift on Valentine's Day. Or try filling a Halloween bag with different kinds of cheese.

You get the idea. It doesn't matter how old you are: chocolate, more than any other food, is special.

Chocolate in most cultures is the very definition of candy. It is a staple of gift giving throughout the year, from Valentine's Day to Easter to Mother's Day to Halloween. Americans eat an average of ten pounds per person per year, while Europeans eat as much as twenty-five pounds. Chocolate candy in all its forms is produced in the billions of pieces. More than eighty million Hershey's Kisses alone are made each and every day. More than one hundred billion M&M's are made each year.

At various times in history, chocolate has been the embodiment of luxury, royalty, privilege, love, and health. Today you can purchase chocolate at conceivably every single grocery, deli, restaurant, convenience store, bakery, pharmacy, gas station, and mall in America.

Cocoa, the ingredient at the heart of chocolate, is one of history's most prized organic substances. Few natural products have been as intensely fought over, and jealously guarded, as cocoa. Once upon a time, it was even used as a form of money, its value greater than gold. Nations have battled over it, families have made astounding fortunes from it, towns have been built around it, movies and books have featured it. It is one of the most precious crops grown on Earth.

Despite its huge popularity, chocolate has rather tiny origins. The story of chocolate starts in rain forests and plantations along the equator, where its creation begins with a fly no bigger than the head of a pin.

WHAT IS CHOCOLATE, REALLY?

ALL CHOCOLATE COMES FROM TREES.

Yes, trees. Chocolate itself doesn't grow on trees, but cocoa does, and cocoa is the primary ingredient in chocolate.

Cocoa comes from the seeds of the cocoa tree (also called the cacao tree), a medium-size tree that grows to a height of about twenty-five feet. The cocoa tree is an extremely sensitive plant. It requires high heat, preferably maintained between 70 and 90 degrees Fahrenheit, as well as a tremendous amount of rain: more than forty-eight inches per year. If any of these conditions are missing, the cocoa tree can't survive. This means that it can only grow naturally on land between a latitude of 20 degrees above and 20 degrees below the equator, where many of the world's rain forests lie.

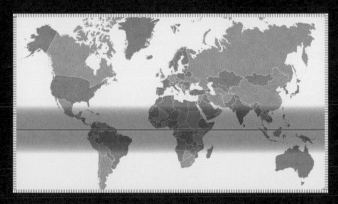

The cocoa tree can only grow in very specific areas of the world, limited to a narrow band above and below the equator.

The cocoa tree has tiny yellow-white and pink flowers that grow right out of the trunk. They bloom all year round. These flowers are barely half an inch in diameter, and in order for the tree to produce seeds, the flowers have to be pollinated. Many of the world's plants are pollinated by bees, butterflies, and birds. But these creatures are too big to crawl into the tiny cocoa flower to deposit pollen. That task can be performed by only one minuscule insect: the midge.

The midge is a fly so small you can barely see it. In fact, it has relatives in North America called "no-see-ums," due to their size. A full-grown midge is barely $1/32$ of an inch long.

In order to stay airborne during flight, the midge's wings must beat an incredible one thousand times per second. (To understand how fast that is, consider this: You can blink your eyes five times a second if you're incredibly quick about it. For each blink, a midge's wings beat two hundred times.)

The midge is barely as big as the head of a pin.

The midge carries pollen from flower to flower, fertilizing the cocoa tree. Only about three flowers out of every thousand manage to grow into a seedpod. This results in about thirty seedpods per tree during each harvesting season. Even though pods grow out from the tree all year round, growers usually pick them during just two or three harvests per year.

These pods are as large as the midge is small. Each seedpod, which grows straight out from the trunk and branches of the tree, is the size and shape of a striped football. Depending on the tree and how ripe the pods are, they can be any number of colors, from orange and gold to bright red and deep purple.

When the pods mature, at about six months, they are cut off the tree by workers using long knives or machetes. Each tree's harvest is piled into an open area, along with pods from other trees. A typical cocoa plantation of just a few acres will produce thousands of pods.

Once the harvest is collected, each pod is split open by hand. Inside the pod are several dozen purple seeds, coated with thick white pulp. The seeds are called cocoa beans and are about the size and shape of almonds.

The beans and pulp are pulled out of the pod. Huge tree leaves, often from banana trees, are laid on the ground, and the cocoa beans and pulp are spread out on top of them. The beans are left to dry on the leaves, but they also begin to ferment, which means their internal chemicals start to break down as they decay. During this fermentation process, the pulp turns into liquid and soaks into the beans. Any excess liquid forms small puddles in the leaves. This liquid is sometimes saved as a slightly sweet fruit juice, but in most cases it is drained off.

Once all the liquid pulp is gone, the beans are left out in the sun to continue drying. After they are thoroughly dried out, they are cracked open. This creates shells and nibs, similar to what you get when you break a peanut out of its shell.

Cocoa pods are roughly the size and shape of a football, and grow in a variety of colors.

A split cocoa pod, revealing the beans coated in white pulp.

The nibs are the heart of the cocoa seed, and the shell is the outer coating. And, as with peanuts, the shell isn't worth much, so shells are sifted to separate them from the nibs.

Now that the nibs are on their own, they are roasted until they become a dark brown color. At this point, they begin to smell something like cocoa. But they are still a long, long way from becoming chocolate.

After they cool, the roasted nibs are ground up between heavy stones. Grinding releases vegetable oil from the nib. This oil is called cocoa butter. As the grinding continues, the friction generates heat. This heat melds the solid pieces of the nib and the cocoa butter together to form a

Above: Cocoa seeds drying in an outdoor rack in Hawaii.

Right: Throughout history, roasted nibs have been ground up with stones to release the cocoa butter.

thick liquid. When the grinding is complete, the liquid is allowed to cool. The liquid hardens and becomes a solid that is called cocoa mass. Only after the mass is formed can cocoa and chocolate products be created.

The mass isn't ready to eat, though. It's not even close, and it actually tastes pretty awful and quite bitter at this stage. It has to go through many more steps to become the chocolate that people crave. Those steps evolved over hundreds of years, developed one bit at a time by ancient civilizations, warriors, scientists, and small family businesses.

COCOA AND THE COKE BOTTLE

The Coca-Cola bottle has one of the most distinctive shapes ever created, familiar to people all over the world.

The secret to that famous contoured shape? The cocoa pod.

In the early 1900s, Coca-Cola was sold in a plain bottle similar to those used by many soda manufacturers. As Coke became popular all across the country, its competitors started naming their products Koke, Koca-Nola, even Cola-Coke. They did this to take advantage of Coke's popularity and to confuse customers. After all, if the bottles looked the same and the names sounded the same, many shoppers would buy a competitor without realizing the difference.

The original Coca Cola bottle.

In 1915, the Coca-Cola company decided to hold a contest to create a bottle so distinctive that any person could always tell it was the real Coca-Cola—even when holding it in the dark. The Root Glass Company of Terre Haute, Indiana, was one of the bottle makers who responded to the challenge.

Several employees of Root Glass went to their local library to learn more about Coke's ingredients, which included the coca leaf and the kola nut. While flipping through encyclopedia entries, the group found an image of a cocoa pod. Cocoa is not an ingredient in Coca-Cola. Yet the indented striations that run the length of the cocoa pod, and its elongated shape, inspired the designers. They gave their Coke bottle a bulge and inserted grooves deep into the glass.

Root Glass won the contest. The result looked very similar to an actual cocoa pod, right down to its thick, rounded middle. Later refinements slimmed the width of the bottle while keeping the vertical lines.

It looks nearly the same today, a full century later. People everywhere recognize the Coke bottle—they just don't know it originated from the same place chocolate does: the cocoa pod.

THE MYSTERIOUS HISTORY OF CHOCOLATE

A GROUP OF RESEARCHERS EXAMINED SOME ancient pottery that had been found along the coast of Honduras, a tiny country in Central America. This particular pottery, which was over three thousand years old, had been used for the serving and drinking of liquids. The researchers discovered that the pottery had traces of cocoa powder in it. This means that humans in the Americas have been grinding cocoa beans to eat or drink for several thousand years.

This pottery dates to the Bronze Age. In that same period, on the other side of the world, the Greeks were fighting the Trojan War, King David was ruling over Israel, and Egypt and Babylon were the most important centers of learning and culture. None of these civilizations had cocoa.

The cocoa tree is native to the rain forests of South America. Before being displaced by people, cities, and farms, it once grew as far north as what

Ancient pottery has been found to contain traces of cocoa.

is now Mexico, so it's not surprising that the first evidence of chocolate use came from people who inhabited Central America. These people learned not only how to turn cocoa seeds into powder but how to tend to the delicate trees. It is likely they created plantations specifically for growing cocoa trees.

A number of advanced civilizations lived in this region of Central America and Mexico, which is known as Mesoamerica. Among them were the Olmecs, the Toltecs, and the Totonacs. We know little about these cultures, because either they had disappeared by the time Europeans settled in Mesoamerica in the early 1500s, or most of the objects and architecture they created at the height of their existence were destroyed during the subsequent Spanish invasion. However, based on artifacts such as the pottery mentioned above, it is likely that these ancient civilizations—especially the Olmecs—were some of the first to harvest cocoa beans and use them for food and beverages.

The main Aztec temple in Mexico City, the center of Mesoamerican culture.

The Mesoamericans that we know the most about, and who are the most important to the story of chocolate, are the Aztecs and the Maya, two civilizations that rose up after the decline of the Olmecs and Toltecs. They were the first large civilizations that the Spanish encountered after Christopher Columbus arrived in the New World in 1492.

The Maya lived along the Yucatán, a large peninsula that juts up into the

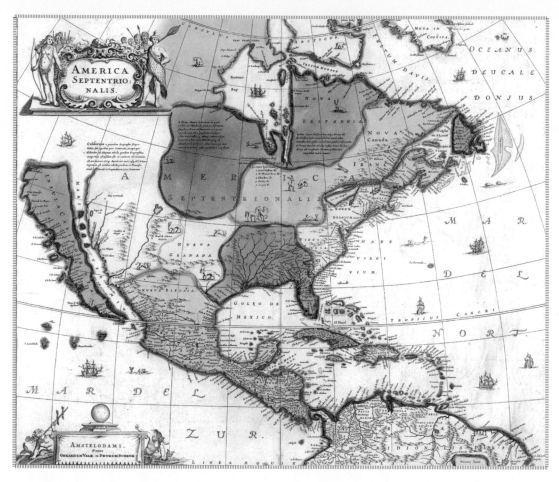

A map of the New World from 1725. Mayan civilization and the Aztec empire covered much of what is now Central America before being conquered by the Spanish.

Gulf of Mexico. As far back as 600 BC, they had created working cocoa plantations by clearing existing forests and planting cocoa trees in their place. They nurtured the trees, harvested the pods, and ground the beans into powder. The powder was mixed with water and spices—including chili, vanilla, dried flower petals, and cornmeal—and served in cups as a beverage.

The drink was made frothy—think of the foam on hot cocoa—by shaking it or blowing air into the bowl. Unlike modern cocoa, though, the cocoa drink the Maya created was bitter; they did not have sugar to sweeten it with. It was also served cool or at room temperature. Nonetheless, cocoa was one of the most important beverages in their society. It marked special occasions, such as religious rituals and holidays. It was also a luxury item, reserved for those who could afford it or those who could trade valuables—like gems—for it.

The Maya called their tree "kawkaw," a word that evolved over the years to become *cocoa*. There has long been confusion about the word *cocoa* and its exact origins. The conquistadors who came upon kawkaw wrote the word in Spanish as *cacao*. When cacao made its way back to Europe, English speakers wrote the word as *cocoa*, or called them *cocow nuts*, adding even more confusion (and they have absolutely no relation to the similar sounding *coconut*). Yet, when Carl Linnaeus, the man who developed the method for classifying living species, named the cocoa tree in 1753, he decided to call it *Theobroma cacao*. *Cacao* came from the original Spanish, while the word *theobroma* is from the Greek for "food of the gods." Obviously, even a scientist like Linnaeus could appreciate the tree's singular importance.

But Linnaeus's naming system meant that many people would call this plant the "cacao tree," while English-speaking countries were already calling it the "cocoa tree." Today both terms are used, although *cocoa tree* is more commonly used when talking about chocolate production. *Cacao* and *cocoa* are thus interchangeable in most cases, but we'll keep it simple in this book by always using the word *cocoa*.

Not only did we get the root word for *cocoa* from the Maya, we also got the word *xocolatl* (pronounced "sho-*co*-lahtl" or "ca-*col*-ahtl"), which some historians think was a native term for the actual drink. The Spanish took their version of this word back to Europe . . . and it eventually became *chocolate*.

The Maya believed that cocoa was a gift from the gods. One of their most important deities, called Ek Chuah, was the god of both war and trade, who protected soldiers as well as merchants. He was portrayed in Mayan art as a dark god with a scorpion tail. Cocoa

Ek Chuah was a Mayan god of war and commerce.

seedpods and beans were offered up to him at festivals, especially by bean sellers and owners of plantations.

Cocoa beans were so valuable to the Maya that they became a form of money. A single bean could buy a vegetable like an onion; ten beans could buy a rabbit. Beans were buried in the tombs of the wealthy and given as gifts and birthday presents.

The Maya were an advanced civilization, one that developed farming techniques and conducted business with other cultures. However, the Maya and many other Mesoamerican nations were dominated by their neighbors to the north: the Aztecs.

The Aztec civilization is legendary, and with good reason. Based in what is now Mexico City, they controlled an empire that extended across thousands of square miles of Mesoamerica. Like the Romans, they built an intricate system of roads to link the parts of their empire. They had very defined social classes, including nobles, soldiers, peasants, and slaves. They were fierce warriors, and forced neighboring nations to submit to their laws and pay taxes to the Aztec government.

The land controlled by the Aztecs was situated north of the Central American tropical forests and those in the Yucatán. It was arid, not suitable for growing plants like the cocoa tree. But because the Aztecs and their ancestors had journeyed south to the land of the Maya, they became enamored of cocoa.

The Aztecs created an impressive and advanced civilization, but they were savage in many of their practices. They believed a constant flow of blood was necessary to keep their gods happy—so their religious rituals included human sacrifice, which involved tearing the hearts out of living victims. During some of the rituals, their sacrifices would be given cocoa—mixed with the blood of previous victims—to energize them and make them more willing to be part of the ceremony.

One of their gods, Quetzalcoatl, was believed to have created the Aztecs by pouring his own blood over the bones of people who had lived hundreds and thousands of years before. Quetzalcoatl was depicted as a feathered serpent, similar to a dragon. According to legend, he came to Earth to serve for a time as an ancient king, and brought with him the knowledge of how to make objects out of gold and silver. He also brought special seeds so that humans could plant the same trees as the gods—cocoa trees—and drink the same cocoa drink that once only the gods had enjoyed.

Aztecs routinely offered human sacrifices to their gods.

Quetzalcoatl was a beloved king, but the other gods grew jealous and wanted him gone. They played a trick on Quetzalcoatl that made him look foolish in front of his people. Embarrassed, he decided to leave Earth. He ascended into the sky, where he became the planet Venus. But before he left, he burned down all the cocoa trees that he had given to mankind, leaving only a few seeds on the shore. This was how the Aztecs explained why they had no cocoa trees in their desert regions, while the forests to the south along the coast did have cocoa.

The Aztecs believed that one day Quetzalcoatl would return and walk among them, and they eagerly awaited that day. In the meantime, they built temples and had feasts to honor him. And they prized his gift of cocoa just as they prized gold and jewels.

Being fearsome and militaristic rulers, the Aztecs expected that those they controlled would regularly bring offerings, or tribute, to keep the peace and show respect to the Aztec leaders. These included a wide range of things such as ornamental pottery, decorative objects, slaves, jaguar skins—and cocoa beans.

Cartloads of the beans were delivered to the Aztec leaders on a regular basis. However, their subjects couldn't produce enough cocoa to meet the demands of the Aztec upper class. To ensure a steady supply, the Aztecs traded for cocoa with the Maya, who were not under their control.

By the year 1500 the Aztecs were the greatest civilization in the Americas. Yet the conquistadors regarded the Aztecs as pagans who would never be as refined or intelligent as the Europeans. Acting on that belief, the Spanish destroyed many of the artifacts of Aztec culture, from books to buildings.

Yet the Spanish were only too happy to keep several Aztec things for themselves. Chief among these things were gold and cocoa.

But we're getting ahead of the story. To find out how cocoa made it from the Aztecs back to Europe, we have go back to the man who started it all. That was Christopher Columbus, who was so unimpressed by a gift of cocoa beans that he tossed them overboard and into the sea.

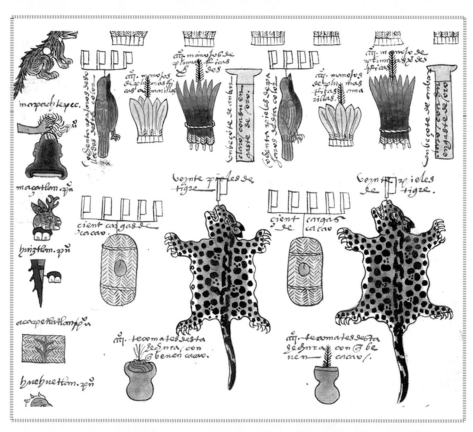

The Codex Mendoza listed the value of Aztec goods, from jaguar skins to sacks of cocoa beans.

COLUMBUS, CORTÉS, CONQUISTADORS, AND COCOA

WHEN CHRISTOPHER COLUMBUS SET OFF in 1492 to sail the ocean blue, no one in Europe knew what he would encounter. His hope was to find a water route to China and India that would increase Spain's business with that part of the world. International trade was becoming increasingly important between nations, as no single country could grow or manufacture everything it needed. The Spanish wanted silk, spices, and tea from Asia, while Asian countries wanted gold and silver from Spain. Getting to Asia faster, and with more goods, would put Spain in a better position than other European countries to get what it wanted from Asia.

A painting of Christopher Columbus, who did not appreciate cocoa beans.

When Columbus reached the Bahamas and Cuba, he at first believed he had made it all the way to the outer edges of India (which is one of the reasons Native Americans were first referred to as Indians). He never expected to run into a land mass located between Europe and India.

As soon as Columbus returned to Spain from his first voyage, he made plans to turn around and go right back to the New World. He wanted to guide dozens of ships and hundreds of people to establish Spanish settlements in the New World, baptize the natives, retrieve valuable gold and cotton, and continue his quest to reach the interior of Asia.

In all, Columbus made four trips to the New World, each time exploring more of the area that would come to be known as Central America (the New World wouldn't come to be known as the Americas until after Columbus died). On his final trip, in 1502, his thirteen-year-old son Ferdinand was with him. They sailed to a small island called Guanaja, which is one of the Bay Islands off the coast of Honduras.

On August 15, native villagers from the island paddled out to Columbus's ship in a long canoe. The canoe was laden with gifts, including a pile of cocoa nibs—something Columbus had never seen before. According to one story, when a handful of the beans was offered to him, Columbus thought they were goat droppings and flung them into the sea. The villagers, shocked by the loss of so many valuable beans, jumped into the water to retrieve as many as they could.

While this account of the first European experience with cocoa is certainly more myth and exaggeration than fact, Ferdinand did later write that cocoa beans were so important to the natives that whenever a bean fell to the deck of the ship "they all stooped to pick it up, as if an eye had fallen."

Whatever the truth of this first meeting between Europeans and the cocoa bean, the Columbus family didn't think much of the little brown seeds. They were more focused on trying to get the local people to lead them to gold mines and convert to Christianity. It's possible that Columbus did not see the locals eat or drink anything made directly from cocoa, so he might have figured it was something used strictly for trade. Columbus is thought to have brought a small amount of cocoa beans back to Spain, but he showed them to the king and queen as an example of the natives' quaint form of money—not as a type of food.

Columbus's trips to the New World led to a veritable Spanish invasion. Famous sailors like Amerigo Vespucci (an Italian navigator hired by Spain, whose name became the basis for "America"), Vasco de Balboa, and Francisco Pizarro all made their way across the Atlantic, as did hundreds of settlers.

The more time the Spanish spent with the natives, the more they realized the importance of the cocoa bean. A detailed description of its use as money was recorded by the writer Gonzalo Fernández de Oviedo, who traveled to the Americas in 1513. In one of his books, he wrote that a human slave could be purchased for one hundred beans—a huge sum.

By 1515 there were Spanish settlements peppered throughout the islands of the Caribbean and the coast of Central America. The Spanish people who moved to the New World started their own farms. They frequently took advantage of native farmers, many of whom were used as slaves. The crops they grew, including sugarcane and cotton, were sent back to Spain. It was the beginning of a huge trade business between Spain and its colonists in the New World.

But there was still much to explore. Very few Spanish settlers had ventured inland toward what the natives called "Mexico"; that territory was uncharted and unknown. Anyone who traveled too far from the coast would likely encounter new and possibly dangerous tribes. With that threat looming, the colonists stayed right where they were. Exploration was left to the true explorers . . . and the conquistadors.

Both explorers and conquistadors were employed in the service of the king and queen of Spain, with one important difference. Explorers, men like Columbus, were typically ship captains and navigators paid to find new lands for Spain to own. Conquistadors, on the other hand, were professional soldiers, men sent to those new lands to make sure that Spain took control of the local people—with military force, if necessary. They were intended to be conquerors. One of the most famous conquistadors was a man named Hernán Cortés.

Hernán Cortés looked for gold, and found cocoa.

A map of Central America with places visited by Cortés.

Cortés was the son of an army officer, and at the age of eighteen went to seek his fortune in the New World. After working for various government officials in different Spanish settlements, Cortés became mayor of Santiago, Cuba's capital city—a prestigious position. But he longed for something more: he had heard rumors and reports of explorers venturing past the Central American beaches and finding gold and silver. Determined to head his own expedition, Cortés managed to get himself appointed to lead an exploration party in 1519 that would venture deeper into Mesoamerica than anyone had before.

When Cortés landed on the Yucatán peninsula, he had two incredible strokes of luck. The first was that he found a Franciscan priest who had learned the Mayan language. Shortly thereafter, Cortés met a native woman who told him about the great and mysterious Aztecs—and she could speak their language. Together these two people could do all of Cortés's translation for him.

The second stroke of luck might have been one of the great coincidences in the history of exploration. The Aztec people believed that their great god Quetzalcoatl, the feathered serpent, would return to them one day, marching back from the seacoast he had left centuries before. The time when the Aztec believed this would happen was the same as the year 1519 on the Spanish calendar.

Cortés had no way of knowing this, but when he chose to search for gold in Mexico, landing on the shore in 1519 with a huge army, all of them dressed in brightly colored clothes and cloaks, he was in the right place at the right time to be mistaken for Quetzalcoatl.

As Cortés marched toward the heart of the Aztec empire, he battled and befriended local tribes—many of whom hated their Aztec rulers—and added their soldiers to his own Spanish troops. By the time he reached the capital of the Aztec world, a magnificent city called Tenochtitlán, Cortés had more than one thousand soldiers with him—along with horses and cannons, which the Aztecs had never seen before.

The ruler of Tenochtitlán was Montezuma, revered as a powerful and savage monarch. Yet upon seeing Cortés's huge army, Montezuma welcomed the conquistador into the city, honoring him with gifts of gold, cotton, jewels, and cocoa beans. Modern historians disagree about whether Montezuma truly believed that Cortés was Quetzalcoatl or whether he was trying to appease Cortés so that he wouldn't destroy the Aztec city with his army. Spanish reports of the time suggest that

Cortés wrecked his own ships so that his soldiers could not abandon his expedition into the Aztec empire.

Cortés was treated as a god and that many Aztecs thought he was the returning Quetzalcoatl. Either way, Montezuma's behavior was considered by Cortés to be a sign of surrender.

One of the luxuries provided for Cortés was the cocoa beverage. Cocoa was served to Cortés and his men in golden goblets with silver stirrers, a sign of its importance. Cortés didn't care for the harshness of the drink, but many of his men became quite fond of it. A writer traveling with Cortés observed: "This is the most healthful and most nutritious food of all known to the world, for one who takes a cup of it, though he may make a long journey, can pass all day without taking another thing." Montezuma was said to drink it dozens of times per day to keep him strong.

Soon, for all intents and purposes, Montezuma became a hostage in his own palace, forced by Cortés to do whatever he was told. This made Cortés the real ruler of the empire, and he was as ruthless as Montezuma. He took many Aztecs as slaves, requiring them to feed and take care of his men. He and his soldiers took whatever gold and riches they could from people all over the Aztec empire, and hoarded it in Tenochtitlán. This led to animosity between the Aztecs and the Spaniards, who increasingly came to distrust each other. When Spanish soldiers attacked and killed some Aztec noblemen during a religious ceremony, it erupted into war.

The war lasted for two years. It was a catastrophe for both sides. The vast riches the Spanish had stolen ended up on the

Montezuma welcomed Cortés into the Aztec capital and then was held hostage in his own city.

bottom of a lake when they unsuccessfully attempted to ship it all out of Tenochtitlán. Many Aztecs died from smallpox they contracted from the Spaniards, a disease against which they had no immunity. Montezuma was killed, and his brother took control of the Aztec army.

Cortés's ships attacked native boats in Tenochtitlán.

In May 1521, the Aztecs were finally overpowered and defeated. As part of the victory celebration, Cortés burned most of their buildings to the ground, destroying much of the great culture's history and the objects they had made. In effect, Cortés put an end to the Aztecs.

The Spanish took total control of Tenochtitlán, which would later be renamed Mexico City. For the next seven years, Cortés governed the Aztec empire, calling it "New Spain." He had nearly everything he could ever want, but the one thing he had come for—vast amounts of gold—had eluded him. However, Cortés was smart enough, some say greedy enough, to see that there was one source of wealth that he *could* control and profit from: the cocoa bean trade.

Not only did natives throughout the New World covet the beans and the drink, but cocoa had become prized by Spanish settlers all over the Americas. Legend has it that nuns in a convent in Oaxaca, a region in southern Mexico, took to adding sugarcane—possibly imported from the island of Cuba—to their cocoa drinks in 1522. This added a sweetness that made the drink even more popular with the Spanish colonists.

Seizing the opportunity, Cortés took over a number of plantations and literally grew his own money. He used the beans to buy goods—including gold, silver, cotton, and corn—from those tribes of Central America that he didn't command. Much of this was shipped back to the royal family in Spain.

In 1528, Cortés himself returned to Spain. He brought boatloads of cocoa beans with him, along with the tools and equipment to grind them and turn them into powder. He also had the ceremonial cups and bowls for serving the cocoa drink. Most important, he had the recipe for making it. Creating the drink was more than just the long process of grinding beans into powder using hand tools: the beans had to be fermented, mashed, sifted, strained, heated, mixed with the right amount of water and spice, and then shaken in a precise way to be turned into a foamy drink.

An illustration from the 1600s showing a man grinding cocoa beans into paste.

Cortés entrusted the recipe to only a few people, notably monks who tweaked the ingredients. They added cinnamon to make cocoa more flavorful when it was served to the Spanish elite. The Spanish also began serving the drink hot, like coffee and tea.

The Spanish in Europe looked on cocoa first and foremost as a potion for keeping them healthy, like a modern vitamin drink. But since cocoa bean supplies were limited—the time between shipments from the Americas could be weeks or months—the drink was extremely expensive. It was something only the wealthiest families could afford. For the same reason, the Spanish did not share cocoa with other countries or their trading partners, fearing that others might try to take the scarce beans for themselves. The Spanish jealously guarded cocoa as their own New World secret.

A RECIPE FOR XOCOLATL

To have a complete chocolate experience, you should taste chocolate the way it was served for hundreds of years in Europe and thousands of years in Central America. The way it was before milk and sugar were added and before it became the basis of the world's favorite candy bar.

There are two ways to go about this. One is time-consuming but will give you a sense of how much effort had to go into its preparation. The other is quick and easy and will taste similar to the first recipe, but will be less true to the original process.

Either way, be prepared. This is not going to taste anything like the chocolate you've come to know and love. In fact, it will be extraordinarily bitter. This chocolate is not an easy drink to like—it is truly an acquired taste—but it has a nice aftertaste once you get past the harshness of the initial sip.

Here are the instructions on how to dive into xocolatl, as it was called in Nahuatl (the language of the Aztecs). We're not going to have you roast and grind your own cocoa beans, so we'll use readily available kitchen ingredients:

> 3 cups water
>
> 1 green chili pepper (Anaheim or jalapeño), sliced
>
> 2 heaping tablespoons unsweetened cocoa powder
> (or unsweetened baking chocolate)*
>
> 1 teaspoon vanilla extract

*If you're using baking chocolate in bar form, you'll have to grate it and mash it with a mortar and pestle to get it close to a powder. You may also substitute solid raw cocoa mass for the unsweetened cocoa powder, and grate that into a powder.

1. Put 1 cup of the water and the sliced chili into a pot. Boil the water for 5 minutes.

2. Remove the water from the pot, then strain it into another pot to remove all the chili solids, like skin and seeds. Put the water back in the original pot, set it to boil, and add the remaining 2 cups of water.

3. As the water is boiling, stir the unsweetened cocoa, unsweetened baking chocolate, or cocoa mass into it.

4. Add vanilla extract. Stir for 5 minutes.

5. Pour the boiling concoction into a mug. Using a small whisk, stir the beverage until it gets frothy (this takes a while). Foam on the top was a big part of the experience, so you should give it a try.

6. Let the drink cool a bit, then sip it.

If you're in a hurry or not interested in the creative process, there's another way to make the drink:

Pour 2 tablespoons of unsweetened cocoa into a mug. Add 1 teaspoon of chili powder. Pour in 1 teaspoon of vanilla. Add 2 cups of boiling water to the mug. Stir it all together briskly until the cocoa powder is dissolved. Let it cool before sipping.

There are many variations of these recipes. You can use less water and get thicker chocolate. You can try getting it to foam by putting it in a container and shaking it. Remember, centuries of experimentation have produced countless variations of the chocolate drink.

Once you've experimented on your own, you can add sugar and milk to taste for yourself how modern hot chocolate—and chocolate milk—came from this strange-tasting drink that is thousands of years old.

The Chocolate Girl.

An eighteenth-century engraving of a girl serving cups of chocolate.

For nearly a hundred years—throughout the 1500s—the Spanish kept cocoa hidden. During that period, other countries sent their own expeditions to the Americas, including England, Italy, Portugal, France, and the Netherlands. Wars broke out as each fought to claim their own parts of the New World.

The warring countries—and the pirates they often employed—were always on the lookout for ships carrying valuables like gold, cloth, and tobacco from America. It is said that on two occasions in the mid-1500s, Spanish ships filled with cocoa beans were captured by the English and the Dutch. Not knowing what the beans were, and mistaking them for sheep droppings (sounds like Columbus's experience, doesn't it?), the English and Dutch sailors sank the Spanish ships. They had no idea they were sending entire fortunes—worth every bit as much as gold—to the bottom of the ocean.

Ongoing battles between European countries eventually provided more nations with access to cocoa.

But, like most secrets, cocoa couldn't stay hidden forever. The first break in Spain's effort to keep the rest of the world away from its beans came in 1606. It was then that a world traveler known as Francesco Carletti made his way back to Italy from the Americas. Carletti was neither an explorer nor a conquistador. Instead, he may have been the world's first tourist, traveling to distant shores on whichever ships would take him. Carletti came into contact with the Maya on one of his trips. He sampled cocoa, and like many before him, fell in love with the drink. When he got back to Italy, he raved about it to his friends in the nobility. Though they couldn't get any cocoa from Spain—which still wasn't admitting it even existed—the Italians were able to get the beans directly from the Americas. They gradually created their own cocoa drink without any help from the Spanish.

A decade later, in 1615, Spain's veil of cocoa secrecy was torn even further. The king of Spain's daughter, Anne, was married off to King Louis XIII of France. Both Anne and Louis were a mere fourteen years old, and Anne had to move to France to be with her new husband. She insisted on having some of her favorite things with her, and that included cocoa. It wasn't long before French royals were all drinking the beverage—and looking for ways to get more of it.

The secret was out. Spain's trading partners demanded access to the beans. Nations at war with Spain stole cocoa from their ships. Spain was also losing its grip on the New World because of uprisings in its territories and constant fighting with other countries, including the Netherlands (where a fondness for cocoa had also arisen). France, too, was aggressively battling Spain in the Americas—and winning. After years of fighting and numerous treaties, France took control of parts of Haiti in 1684 and established cocoa plantations there. This gave the French their own direct supply of the beans, without having to rely on Spain.

The Spanish stranglehold on the cocoa trade, and its role in the development of chocolate, was brought to an end by Dutch merchants. The Dutch were the leading traders in the world during the 1600s and 1700s. They built warehouses in Amsterdam that allowed many countries to do business in a single central port. Amsterdam and its docks became a hub for goods from every part of the world. Wine from France could be loaded onto a ship with olives from Italy and beef from Spain, and then shipped to England or India or Mexico. Although many European countries were at war, the Dutch traders were able to keep international business going while kings and queens squabbled with each other.

Left: *The Dutch West Indies Flag.*

Below: *The Dutch West Indies headquarters in Amsterdam.*

HET WEST INDISCH HUYS.

The Dutch had two large companies that handled a great deal of this international trade: the Dutch East India Company, which dealt with Asia, and the Dutch West India Company, which worked with the Americas. The latter company set up a port with warehouses on the Caribbean island of Curaçao to handle goods coming out of Central and South America. Much of this was cocoa, which the Dutch were more than happy to sell to those countries that Spain wouldn't. And with the Dutch West India Company's connections all over the New World, it had a regular supply of the beans to ship back to Europe.

By the beginning of the eighteenth century, Spain was weakened by ongoing wars, and its global power had waned to the point where it was no longer a factor in the cocoa business. Now it was up to other countries to turn the cocoa plant and its seeds into the chocolate we know today.

MAIN COCOA-GROWING REGIONS

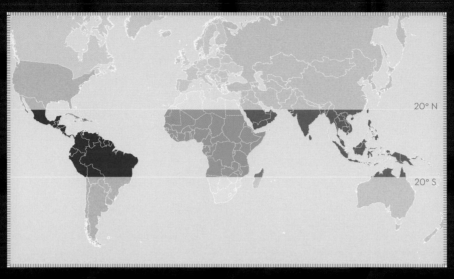

20° N

20° S

Africa: 71.2%   Americas: 15.3%   Asia and Oceania: 13.5%

LARGEST PRODUCERS OF COCOA

Cote d'Ivoire: 1,700,000 tons

Ghana: 820,000 tons

Indonesia: 350,000 tons

Cameroon: 320,000 tons

Ecuador: 230,000 tons

Nigeria: 220,000 tons

Brazil: 200,000 tons

Papua New Guinea: 35,000 tons

The list to the left shows the countries that produce most of the worlds cocoa beans. Other countries that grow cocoa are Belize, Bolivia, Colombia, Costa Rica, Cuba, the Democratic Republic of the Congo, the Dominican Republic, Fiji, Grenada, Haiti, Hawaii (United States), Madagascar, Malaysia, Mexico, Peru, the Philippines, the Seychelles, Sierra Leone, Sri Lanka, Togo, Trinidad, Venezuela, and Vietnam.

Total produced: four million tons annually

PRESSING CHOCOLATE FROM A BEAN

DEMAND FOR COCOA WAS WIDESPREAD THROUGH-out Europe, despite more than a hundred years of tightfisted control by Spain. Europeans had developed a taste for cocoa as far back as the late 1500s, yet they discovered it in vastly different ways. The Germans and Austrians learned of cocoa from the little shops that appeared throughout Italy in the years after Francesco Carletti brought cocoa back from his travels. The Swiss got it when the mayor of Zurich, Heinrich Escher, sampled cocoa in Belgium and took some home. Belgium had access to cocoa because it was ruled by Spain. Colonials in North America import-ed cocoa directly from colonies in Central America. The English got their supply by trading with the Dutch, and also from an enterprising Frenchman who had opened a club in his London house in 1567. The club served coffee, tobacco, and cocoa. This gathering spot, primarily for wealthy men, may have been the first public place to sell cocoa to anyone who could afford it.

A seventeenth-century engraving depicts the popularity of cocoa in cultures around the world.

As countries sought larger supplies of cocoa, more plantations were created in the Americas. Production of the beans increased to keep up with European demand. Since there was more cocoa to go around, the price dropped—a little. This didn't mean that everyone could afford cocoa, which was still consumed primarily for health and relaxation. Most cocoa was served in small cafés or restaurants; you couldn't go to a market and buy cocoa to make at home. Besides, most people would not have known how to prepare the drink. The intricate mixing, while no longer a secret, still required complex preparation.

One group that did not get to taste cocoa was children. It cost so much that adults had to think twice before buying it for themselves, and even wealthy adults would not have given such an extravagant treat to kids. The French king Louis and his bride, Anne, were some of the only European children to have experienced expensive cocoa between 1600 and 1700.

The marriage of King Louis XIII to Anne in 1615.

There was one region of the world where cocoa wasn't just a drink for the rich and powerful. That was in the colonies of North America. People there gave little thought to their kings and queens—as would be proven during the Revolutionary War in the late 1700s. Thus there was much less class distinction between rich and poor than there was in Europe. Cocoa was expensive, but not so much that it was solely a moneyed man's drink. Because there was a brisk shipping trade between places like New England and New York and the cocoa growers in Central America, cocoa was more readily available and quicker to come by than it was for people across the Atlantic Ocean.

Cities in New England became known

for their cocoa production, especially Boston; Providence; and New Haven, Connecticut. The latter town was home to a cocoa seller named Benedict Arnold, who would become notorious in his lifetime for selling something other than cocoa—namely, secrets to the enemy.

The biggest seller of cocoa products in the North American colonies was a man named Dr. James Baker. He had built a factory in Dorchester, Massachusetts, in 1765, a full decade before the signing of the Declaration of Independence. The factory was attached to an old sawmill that had pressing equipment—which he used to smash his cocoa beans.

Baker was a pioneer in the concept of marketing, and advertised "Baker's cocoa" throughout the colonies. He was also a stickler for quality, insisting on getting the best beans from his suppliers and never using hidden "fillers." (Some cocoa makers dishonestly added potato flour or powdered cocoa shells to their "pure cocoa" to cut costs.) To keep up with the demand, Baker and his son Edmund took over other mills in New England and converted them to chocolate production. Soon the Baker Company was producing tons of cocoa every month.

While New England cocoa makers were fortunate to get speedy shipments of cocoa, getting cocoa to Europe was a time-consuming and expensive proposition. Traders transporting cocoa nibs and beans to Europe realized that they could cram more cocoa into their ships if they reduced it to exactly what their customers wanted. This meant getting rid of the shells and grinding down the nibs before they loaded the ships so that they were only transporting blocks of cocoa mass—the end product itself. Not only did this allow for more cocoa on board, but it also made it easier for shopkeepers and café owners to produce cocoa drinks. They no longer had to do their own grinding and separating but could simply scrape or grate the cocoa mass to make their drinks. If they had enough on hand, the cafés would sell part of their solid cocoa to anyone who wanted to make the beverage at home.

With more and more people drinking and buying cocoa, new businesses dedicated to all things cocoa grew up throughout Europe and America.

An eighteenth-century painting of a mother and daughter enjoying cocoa.

Craftsmen made the special grinding tools used by restaurants for powdering the cocoa mass; others made the unique pots used to heat it up and add froth; tradesmen offered to grind cocoa for people who didn't have the proper tools in their home; and still others created small silver or porcelain drinking cups and saucers specifically for drinking cocoa. The tiny saucers caught every drop and prevented the dark liquid from dripping and staining clothes and tablecloths.

Throughout the 1700s, cocoa itself didn't change much. It was still a very bitter drink. The English took to adding milk, just as they did with their tea. The Italians added different spices, as well as crushed flower petals, to their version. It was sold in restaurants, pharmacies, cafés, and chocolate shops that resembled today's coffee shops. By and large, no one thought about eating it.

The first changes to the notion of cocoa as simply an expensive drink came when shopkeepers and chefs began experimenting with it. Italian bakers, long known for inventing unique and delicious pastries, started adding ground cocoa to their creations. It was not sweet, but it added a novel taste to desserts. Bakers in other countries, notably France and Belgium, also began adding cocoa to existing foods—from breads to pastas—and mixing it into sauces or sprinkling it into ice cream.

Part of the reason for this experimentation was an eighteenth-century French invention: machine presses that could smash the cocoa in minutes, cutting many hours off the time it took to do it by hand. The process required fewer workers, so cocoa could be prepared more rapidly and at a lower price. By the end of the 1700s, cocoa was cheap enough that it became readily available to the public. People could buy chunks of cocoa mass from pharmacists or bakers who chopped it off larger blocks—almost as if they were selling slices of cheese.

One of the first people to take advantage of this was François-Louis Cailler. Born in Switzerland, he had lived in Turin, Italy, for several years, and learned how to make cocoa according to an Italian recipe that blended spices into the mass. When he returned to Switzerland, he decided to produce cocoa on a large scale, much larger than what individual boutiques or cafés or restaurants could grind out themselves. He built an actual chocolate factory—with crushing machines that used huge stone rollers—that turned out hundreds of pounds of cocoa mass every year. This was the first highly mechanized production of cocoa and, as is true of almost all mass production, it reduced the cost even further.

Left: François-Louis Cailler.

Below: Coenraad Van Houten.

Shopkeepers immediately began buying his cocoa mass to save themselves the trouble of grinding their own beans.

To ensure that people from all walks of life could purchase the cocoa, Cailler started producing his cocoa mass in very small bricks—or bars—that made cocoa even more affordable. These were the first chocolate bars, although they were still used for making drinks.

The most important invention in the history of cocoa—and the one that leads us directly to the chocolate we know today—came from a man named Coenraad Van Houten. A chemist living in Amsterdam in the 1820s, Van Houten worked in his father's cocoa company. To grind their cocoa, the Van Houtens used a huge stone mill, operated by men forcing stone rollers over the nibs. This was labor intensive, and while it was faster than hand grinding, the cocoa mass was the same quality as if it had been done by hand. Van Houten wanted cocoa with a stronger flavor, which he realized meant getting rid of some of the cocoa butter while retaining all the solid pieces of the nib. He devised a more powerful machine to press the nibs, forcing more of the cocoa butter away from the paste.

Here's where we have to take a step away from our history and learn a little bit about chocolate chemistry. That's because we've reached the point where cocoa went from being something people drank to something people ate.

Let's look at the process of creating cocoa. The roasted nibs, which are nearly as hard as little pebbles, are ground down. As they are ground, the natural vegetable oil in the nibs, known as cocoa butter, is released as a liquid and mixes with the granules from the solid part of the nib. When this mixture cools, it becomes the cocoa mass (some makers call it "chocolate liquor," although it has nothing to do with alcohol or cocktails and is not a liquid). Think of the mass as being similar in hardness and consistency to a big wax candle. It is made of 53 percent cocoa butter and 47 percent solids from the nib. It is bitter to the taste, with nothing sweet about it. To get a sense of just how bitter it is, taste a tiny bit of unsweetened baking chocolate or cocoa powder. Only a little—it is not pleasant to modern taste buds.

It is this waxy cocoa mass—part cocoa butter, part nib solids—that was used for cocoa drinks. What made preparing the drinks so difficult was that the oily cocoa butter, which is a type of fat, would not mix easily with water. (Oil and water don't mix, as you probably know; the oil quickly separates from the water.)

To help the mix along, the cocoa mass was often boiled in water, and as the cocoa butter separated from the mass, the oil was skimmed off the top of the water. Eventually, enough boiling and skimming reduced the fatty oil. What was left was a solid that could be grated, ground, or pounded, and then mixed into water as a drink. Drinks in some shops and homes were served without going through this process, leaving a greasy layer of cocoa butter floating on the top. Needless to say, it wasn't appetizing—and the vegetable fat made the cocoa drink hard to digest.

The Van Houtens knew that if they could remove as much of the cocoa butter as possible during the grinding process, it would make for a purer cocoa mass. Plus, it would save time during the boil-and-skim process.

They created an intricate mechanical press that was powered by a windmill. As the windmill turned, it rotated the press downward with incredible force. It was strong enough to squeeze more cocoa butter than ever before out of the nibs. When the Van Houtens ground the nibs as much as they could, the remaining cocoa mass was only 27 percent cocoa butter. They had managed to reduce the amount of cocoa butter in the cocoa mass by half. There were now more nib solids in the cocoa mass than there was cocoa butter.

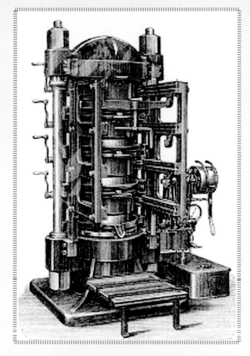

An early Van Houten cocoa press.

Now, this doesn't sound like a very big deal. Reduce the fat—so what? But it changed the nature of cocoa. With less oil, the cocoa mass was drier and could be pulverized into a powder. This powder could be easily stirred into water, making the creation of a cocoa drink something anyone could do.

The Van Houten press and their process, which was patented as a new invention in 1828, was a great stride in making cocoa cheap and easy to make. When the Van Houtens processed a load of cocoa beans, here is what they created:

COCOA MASS: A paste that was a mixture of cocoa butter and cocoa solids. It was just like the mass many generations of cocoa makers had made before them. But then the Van Houtens smashed it again, squeezing more cocoa butter out of it. That gave them two things . . .

COCOA CAKE: A dry cocoa mass that has nothing to do with cake as we know it; it's just a name for the mass after more cocoa butter was squeezed out. For this reason, it is also called a press cake. This cake could be broken up into a light and fluffy cocoa powder. What was left over was . . .

COCOA BUTTER: The part of the prepared cocoa bean that had previously been skimmed off and discarded. It was like other types of fats and oils, and resembled an ivory-colored butter. It was creamy and pourable when in liquid form, and almost solid when cool. Of particular note was that it didn't melt at room temperature like dairy butter, but had a higher melting point of nearly 90 degrees Fahrenheit, which was closer to human body temperature. As an added benefit, it didn't spoil quickly—it could be stored for months without going bad.

Cocoa mass on the left, is ground down to cocoa cake (center) and cocoa butter (right).

Using his training as a chemist, Coenraad Van Houten went to work making the most out of his new products. The first thing he did was add a special kind of salt—called alkali salt—to the cocoa cake. Chemically, this counteracted much of the bitterness in cocoa's taste, made it much darker, and helped it dissolve almost completely in liquid (much like the cocoa powder you use for making hot chocolate or chocolate milk). Van Houten's unique dark cocoa soon became known as Dutch chocolate.

The ready availability of Dutch chocolate powder led to its use in things besides the cocoa drink. It was added to coffee as well as to baked goods like pastries and cookies. (Certain modern foods, especially baked and packaged goods like Oreos, are nearly black due to the "Dutch" process of creating chocolate.)

But cocoa powder wasn't the only thing brought about by the windmill press. Of more importance was all that leftover cocoa butter that had been squeezed out of the cocoa mass. It didn't have the full flavor of the cocoa cake, but it had interesting physical properties. No one realized how important cocoa butter was, not even Coenraad Van Houten. But it was expensive, as all things related to cocoa beans were, so cocoa makers were reluctant to throw it away. After Van Houten's method caught on, various food producers tried to figure out what to do with the cocoa butter—attempting to use it as a substitute for other vegetable and animal fats like olive oil and dairy butter—but nothing came of it. At first.

Interestingly, some people found that cocoa butter worked pretty well as a lotion when it was rubbed on dry skin, since it melted at body temperature. Today, cocoa butter is used in a huge number of cosmetic products.

Other chocolate makers throughout Europe followed Van Houten's lead and squeezed more cocoa butter out of their cocoa mass. Cocoa powder became cheap enough that people could afford to have it in their kitchens. This was especially true in England, where cocoa had already been less of a luxury item than it was in other countries, and now became more like tea and coffee—although it was still relatively expensive, as the government put a heavy tax on it. Cocoa was served like tea and coffee, with milk and sugar frequently added to it.

Cocoa in England was originally dispensed by pharmacies—called apothecaries—since the drink was used for medicinal and health purposes. Many doctors prescribed it, believing that it cured everything from upset stomachs and cholera to nervousness and fatigue. As the demand for cocoa increased, some of these apothecaries grew into businesses that specialized only in cocoa.

One was owned by Joseph Storrs Fry, whose father had been among the first chocolate makers in Britain. Fry was a Quaker, a religious group that opposed the drinking of alcohol, believing that it contributed to many social problems.

Fry felt that by offering cocoa to his customers, he was providing an alternative to going to pubs, and thus helping society. One of his competitors, a man named John Cadbury, who owned a business that sold cocoa along with tea and coffee, was also a Quaker.

Fry invented a way to use a steam engine to press his cocoa, and by the 1820s, his company was the biggest chocolate maker in England. He sold his chocolate to dozens of apothecaries, cafés, and restaurants all over the country.

Like the Van Houtens', Fry's company was a family affair, run by Joseph and his three boys under the name J. S. Fry and Sons. And, like the Van Houtens, the Frys were left with a lot of cocoa butter they didn't need after grinding their mass. The Fry boys, after their father's death in 1835, tried to find a way to make use of the cocoa butter.

The details of what happened next are lost to history, but we can venture a guess at how the Frys made a decision that would change the way in which cocoa was used forever. On the one hand, they had this marvelous cocoa powder that mixed with just about everything and had a strong flavor. On the other hand, they had this buttery substance that was creamy, long lasting, and didn't taste like much of anything, although it had the aroma of cocoa.

What would happen if some of the flavorful cocoa powder was mixed back into the creamy cocoa butter?

The answer was the first chocolate for eating.

The Frys found that the two products, after they'd already been separated, created something truly unique when combined back together. It was still unsweetened and somewhat harsh, but it had a nice texture, melted in the mouth, and could be eaten anywhere. Even better, given its softness at high temperatures, it could be pressed into molds like a thick mud or paste. After it

The J. S. Fry and Sons factory in Bristol, England.

cooled, the Frys' chocolate could be removed from the molds and sold in small individual pieces.

In 1847, the Fry company introduced a product called Chocolat Délicieux à Manger (a French name that translates to "delicious chocolate to eat"). It was the first chocolate bar. And people liked it.

Fry's competitors also liked it. Very quickly, other cocoa makers introduced their own chocolate bars, especially John Cadbury, who started advertising his brand of chocolate all over England. Competition became fierce. To distinguish themselves from each other, the companies added different spices and flavorings like sugar, cinnamon, or vanilla to their recipes. Some didn't add anything, advertising their products as "pure."

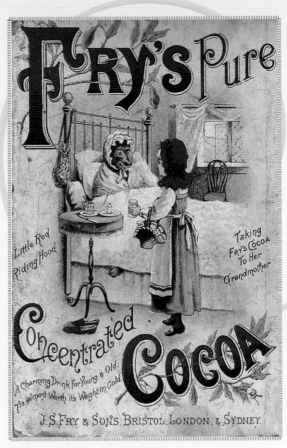

An early Fry's ad showing Red Rising Hood delivering a basket of cocoa to her "grandmother."

The chocolate bar was born, thanks to the Fry boys. But it still wasn't "candy" or any type of confection. ("Confection" is an all-purpose term for sweets, including candy, cakes, and cookies.) The bars didn't have enough sugar to make them sweet, and they were intended—like cocoa drinks—primarily for adults. The new "eating chocolate" wasn't marketed as a treat, either. Real treats were cookies, caramels, nuts coated with icing, or sugar plums and other hard sugar concoctions. Chocolate was considered more like a unique health food than any type of sweet.

So it remained until the 1870s. That was when a man making chocolate met up with a pharmacist making baby food. After they helped save a little girl's life, they created the world's most popular treat.

5

CHOCOLATE MEETS MILK—BY WAY OF BABY FORMULA

HERE WE REACH ANOTHER TURNING POINT IN the history of chocolate. Going forward, almost every chocolate development involves families—not tribes or kings and queens or huge companies, but family-run businesses. Most of these families started out in their kitchens or a small room with ovens and stoves and boiling pots. Dining room tables and home mixing machines were their "factories." Family members, no matter how young or old, usually pitched in to stir, mix, bake, cook, and wrap the chocolate.

At the same time, the way the words *cocoa* and *chocolate* were used came to mean different things. The word *cocoa* would refer to the powder used for making a beverage, as well as the powder used for baking. *Chocolate* would mean anything related to a product made from the mixture of cocoa butter and cocoa powder, as well as the product used to flavor other foods, such as chocolate frosting or chocolate syrup. People

A 1742 French illustration of a cocoa tree.

drank cocoa or *baked* with it. Chocolate was the thing you *ate*.

Because different chocolate makers in different countries were trying different things with chocolate during the 1800s, it's easy to forget that many of these countries were often at war with each other. The very young United States was fighting several European countries, including England and Spain, not to mention having its own Civil War. And the South American colonies established by European nations were angry—like the United States had been—at being ruled by kings and queens from afar. Most notable of these was Brazil, which was tired of being governed by Portugal and wanted its independence.

At the same time, many European countries were exploring Africa and the lands of Southeast Asia and setting up colonies there. For Europeans, the African continent was more appealing than the Americas because it was geographically closer. Africa offered new opportunities to obtain natural resources, establish plantations, and increase the size of their empires.

Portugal, being just across the Strait of Gibraltar, was quick to establish a presence in Africa. Perhaps sensing that they wouldn't be able to hold on to Brazil much longer (they weren't), the Portuguese shipped cocoa plants to the tiny islands of São Tomé and Príncipe off the west

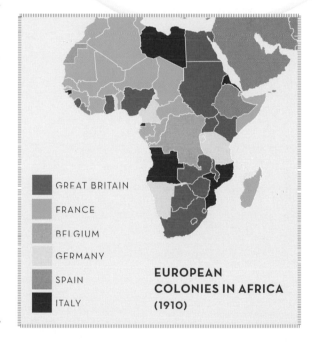

GREAT BRITAIN

FRANCE

BELGIUM

GERMANY

SPAIN

ITALY

EUROPEAN COLONIES IN AFRICA (1910)

coast of Africa. There they created new plantations—the first time the cocoa plant was ever grown outside of Central and South America. Since the climate along the coast of equatorial Africa was very similar to that of the Americas, complete with tropical rain forests, the cocoa plant adapted easily.

Other countries, specifically the Netherlands and Belgium, developed their own cocoa plantations in Africa. The rulers of these nations preferred Africa for the cocoa trade instead of the Americas, because it took less time for the cocoa to be shipped home, and because they could use slave labor. The unfortunate fact of the 1800s and much of the 1900s was that slaves were used to work the crops in many European colonies.

It wasn't long before cocoa was being grown in the African colonies that would become Ghana, Guinea, Cameroon, Nigeria, Cote d'Ivoire, and Sierra Leone. The English, who ruled the seas at the time, took cocoa plants from the Americas all the way to India, Ceylon, Singapore, and even Australia—all British colonies—to have their own source of beans.

GREAT BRITAIN

FRANCE

NETHERLANDS

EUROPEAN COLONIES IN THE INDIAN AND PACIFIC OCEANS (1926)

Even as the number of places growing cocoa expanded, the demand kept increasing—for the drink. Despite the introduction of edible chocolate, it was the cocoa beverage that most people spent their money on. Besides, the cocoa drink was evolving into a sweet of its own. The English and the Swiss were adding sugar and milk to their powdered cocoa, making it a drink that tasted good to almost everyone—while increasing the demand for cocoa even more.

Coincidentally, as science improved in the late 1800s, doctors realized that cocoa was not quite the wondrous medical potion that it had been promoted as. Like a few other beverages, including coffee, it had a bit of a kick to it, but that didn't improve the drinker's overall health. That really didn't matter so much, as people now drank it because they thought it tasted delicious.

The addition of sugar and milk to cocoa drinks made chocolate makers realize that doing the same thing to solid chocolate might improve its popularity. Adding sugar to cocoa butter was a simple process, although it made the chocolate gritty, since the sugar granules didn't dissolve. But there was a bigger problem: it was nearly impossible to mix cocoa butter with milk.

Milk is a unique combination of fat and water. We get things like cream, butter, and cheese by removing certain amounts of either the fat or the water from milk. The less fat, the more liquid it becomes—skim milk, for example. More fat means it's less liquid, like cream, or even butter.

When they tried mixing milk with cocoa butter, chocolate makers saw that the fatty parts of the two melded, but the water did not. Almost all the water separated from the fat—but tiny bits still remained inside the actual chocolate, causing it to become rancid.

A man who worked on trying to solve this problem was a Swiss candle maker named Daniel Peter. When the introduction of oil lamps ruined the candle industry in the mid-1800s, Peter had to look for some other line of business to pursue. During his years at the candle company, he had fallen in love with and married Fanny Cailler, who was the eldest daughter of François-Louis Cailler. Her father, you might recall, was credited with creating the first chocolate bar and spearheading the mass production of cocoa. Even though François had passed away several years earlier, Peter became very interested in chocolate and committed himself to finding a way to make milk chocolate in solid form. It helped that he was living in Switzerland, a country that prided itself on the quality and quantity of the milk from its dairy cows.

As happened to so many before him, though, his efforts met with failure. Milk just didn't blend with solid chocolate. Try as he might, nothing worked. In 1867, Peter was also distracted by problems in his personal life. His wife had just given birth to their daughter, Rose, and the baby was having difficulty breast-feeding. There weren't many baby food options available for Rose. Peter was concerned that his daughter would get sick and die from starvation.

Daniel Peter.

Peter mentioned the feeding problem to his neighbor, Henri Nestlé. A pharmacist who had moved to Switzerland from his native Germany, Nestlé owned a business that produced a variety of beverages, from mineral water and lemonade to alcohol-based liquors. One of his personal interests was trying to create a liquid baby food that could be used as an alternative to breast milk.

Henri had been one of fourteen children, and half of his brothers and sisters had died while young. He was very aware of the problem of giving babies proper nutrition to make sure they survived past their infancy.

Henri Nestlé.

Infant mortality at the time claimed nearly one out of every five children, with malnutrition being one of the biggest factors. While breast milk was always the preferred food, babies who wouldn't or couldn't drink it were in danger of dying from malnutrition. People tried cow's or goat's milk as a substitute, but it was hard for babies to digest. To make matters worse, little attention was paid to hygiene in the 1800s, so animal milk could be easily contaminated, and thus deadly to babies.

For years, Nestlé experimented with ways to create a baby food that was similar to mother's milk. In 1866, he created a formula made from powdered cow's milk, wheat flour, sugar, and water. By removing the starch and acid from the flour, and using milk powder instead of whole milk, he made the resulting liquid easy to digest and provided babies with much-needed nutrition. The world didn't know it at the time, but Nestlé had created both infant formula and baby food.

Very few mothers, however, were willing to feed their sick babies a new and untested product. Some did try Nestlé's formula, but not enough to make it a success.

In an odd turn of events, Nestlé heard of a baby boy born prematurely in a nearby town who was unable to eat any type of food. The baby was so sick that he was convulsing. Doctors had determined there was no hope and had stopped treating him. Nestlé went to see the parents and provided them with his new formula. The desperate parents were willing to try anything. To their surprise, the baby took the food. Within several weeks he had recovered and was completely healthy. His parents were ecstatic. The story of Nestlé's formula saving the baby spread throughout Switzerland, and then Europe. Soon doctors and nurses were requesting it.

But that particular success and Nestlé's fame were still in the future. Right now, Daniel Peter's daughter was very sick, and he was asking for Henri's help.

It was an early version of his formula that Nestlé offered to Peter in 1867, but it worked, and baby Rose was nursed back to health. While she was recovering, the two men struck up a friendship. Having similar interests in milk and its properties, they shared stories of their experiments. After many discussions, Peter believed that if he could mix a form of powdered milk similar to that created by Nestlé into his chocolate, he would be able to overcome the problem of water ruining chocolate.

It was more complicated than just mixing all the ingredients together. The milk and the chocolate had to be mixed in the correct amount, then heated together at the correct temperature and at the correct moment. Otherwise, the batch would be ruined.

Peter struggled for years, experimenting on his own to come up with the right proportions. In the meantime, Henri Nestlé's baby formula became a worldwide success. In 1875, Nestlé sold his company, making him very rich. (Oddly, given all the things he had done to help make babies healthy, Nestlé and his wife were never able to have children of their own.)

Now that he was retired, Nestlé aided Peter when he could. The two men examined the problems Peter was having with getting the ingredients to meld together. They determined that Peter should use condensed milk instead of powdered milk. (Condensed milk is a form of milk that has much of the water taken out of it but is still a liquid—it is sold in small cans today and commonly used for baking.) Interestingly, one of Nestlé's biggest competitors was the company that made the best condensed milk, so Peter used their milk. It made no difference to Henri what brand Peter used; Henri was retired and no longer worked for the company that bore his name.

Peter combined cocoa butter, cocoa powder, sugar, and the condensed milk at a precise temperature to make a syrupy concoction that finally did everything he wanted it to. The year was 1875, and it had taken Peter eight years since his first meeting with Nestlé to perfect his product. He had hit on a chocolate formula that featured the best of everything that had come before. He called it *chocolat au lait*, which translates to "milk chocolate." It was smooth, creamy, sugary, and full of cocoa flavor.

His original formula was welcomed as a sweet drink. People still wanted their chocolate the way they had their cocoa—in a cup or a mug or a glass—

Packaging for Daniel Peter's new "milk" chocolate.

and Peter was happy to sell it that way. He promoted his milk chocolate all over Europe, winning awards at exhibitions for his new "food invention." He was aided by his country's location as an international crossroads: Switzerland is conveniently tucked between Italy, France, Germany, and Austria. In addition, its renowned schools—the fabled Swiss boarding schools—were attracting students and their families from places as far away as England and even America.

Peter formed a company called Peter-Cailler, which became the world's first purveyor of milk chocolate. It became especially popular in England, another place where people prized their milk and their cows. Soon consumers wanted the creamy, rich Peter-Cailler chocolate for more than just drinking; they wanted it as a dessert and for special occasions.

There was one more big invention needed to turn chocolate permanently from a drink to a candy. That was a machine called the conch. Rodolphe Lindt, a young Swiss man from a wealthy family, enjoyed the milk chocolate made by Peter-Cailler. But even with the improvements that Daniel Peter had made, Lindt thought more could be done. There was still the tiniest bit of water in Peter's milk chocolate, and it caused some crystallization. The crystallization made the chocolate gritty. And, in some batches, the amount of milk overshadowed the chocolate itself, taking away from the cocoa flavor and aroma.

Lindt set out to make chocolate even better. There arc claims that he decided to get into the chocolate business as a hobby, since his family was already wealthy. It's possible, but he was determined nonetheless. He trained as a confectioner's apprentice with Charles-Amédée Kohler, a relative who had gained fame for blending hazelnuts into his cocoa. After four years with Kohler, Lindt decided to start his own company.

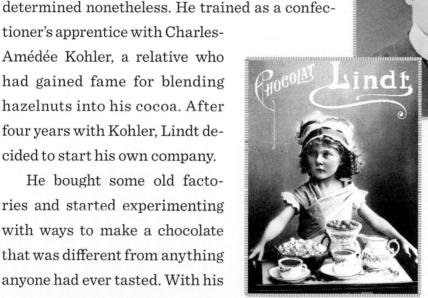

He bought some old factories and started experimenting with ways to make a chocolate that was different from anything anyone had ever tasted. With his brother August, a pharmacist, he spent months and months subjecting milk chocolate to all sorts of tests. The Lindts discovered that repeated stirring of cocoa butter with condensed milk, sugar, and cocoa powder added air to the mixture, which released some of the milky odor and concentrated the cocoa scent. The stirring and blending also reduced the grittiness to almost nothing. To automate the stirring process,

Above: Rodolphe Lindt.

Left: An advertisement for Lindt's unique chocolate.

Rodolphe created a machine that looked like a big conch shell. It was capable of swirling chocolate about for hours.

What happened next was either deliberate planning or an accident; Lindt never revealed which. One weekend in 1879 the conch machine was left on for three days. Those who believe Lindt was just in the chocolate business as a lark claim he simply went on vacation and didn't bother to turn it off. Others claim he had finally figured out the perfect amount of time to "conch" his chocolate. Either way, Lindt returned to his factory and found that the nonstop stirring and rolling had produced the chocolate of his dreams. It was perfectly smooth, poured like a syrup when warm, smelled like sugar and cocoa, and tasted unlike anything he or anyone else had ever tasted.

Rodolphe created a machine that had internal mechanisms resembling a big conch shell.

Having created a wonderfully edible form of chocolate, Lindt began making small batches for sale. He wasn't really interested in growing his business into a big company and didn't bother advertising or hiring salespeople. It is said he only sold to people he liked. But people who tasted his chocolate sought him out and demanded—perhaps begged—for more.

Lindt's ability to pour chocolate—in its liquid form—meant that it could be put into molds and then cooled, making hundreds of small chocolates at a time. It could also be warmed up and squeezed into pastries or drizzled onto cakes and cookies. There was almost nothing that chefs, bakers, cooks, and people at home wouldn't try with Lindt's chocolate.

Seeing that he had something revolutionary on his hands, Lindt kept his process secret. He locked his factories and hid his machines from visitors. He refused to divulge the recipe to anyone. For twenty years, his competitors tried to figure out what he'd done to create such an amazing confection. Magazines and newspapers even speculated as to what was behind the recipe.

Lindt kept the process of conching secret for two decades, only revealing it in 1899 when he sold his company. The new

*Wrapper for
Lindt's Swiss chocolate.*

owners also guarded the secret, but—like many secrets—the details of conching eventually slipped out. Within a decade, the entire chocolate business was conching its chocolate . . . and does so to this day.

Thanks to Daniel Peter and Rodolphe Lindt, milk chocolate became Europe's most sought-after sweet. It was not only loved by consumers, it was loved by the companies that made it. Adding milk—which was cheap—to the chocolate process meant that the amount of cocoa butter and cocoa powder could be reduced. Milk chocolate made dairy farmers incredibly happy: they found a whole new industry that would buy their milk. Shopkeepers were eager to sell this new product that all their customers were demanding. It seemed that everyone who came into contact with milk chocolate benefited from it.

In its newest form, chocolate was destined to become the world's favorite flavor, something used in every form of dessert and candy imaginable. After nearly four hundred years of using the cocoa bean for drinks—in all its bitterness and complicated preparation—Europeans could now simply walk into a store and buy an astoundingly delicious bit of chocolate made from those same beans.

It had been a long and unusual path, but chocolate had arrived.

The twentieth century was dawning. Europe had long led the evolution of chocolate, but now American chocolate makers would take their turn in the spotlight. They would show the world what the United States could do. And the wars between the world's chocolate families would begin.

6

ALL IN THE FAMILY

Baker's Chocolate was one of the first cocoa producers in the United States.

AT THE START OF THE TWENTIETH CENTURY, "sweet to eat" chocolate was all the rage throughout Europe. Each country had its favorite type of chocolate, based largely on which company was the biggest chocolate seller in the nation. And each seller had achieved popularity thanks to the individual way in which they produced their chocolate. They all had secret recipes that ranged from the temperature at which nibs were roasted and how much sugar was added to the cocoa butter to how long the chocolate was conched and how quickly it was cooled.

None of these was the single "right" recipe: all of them were considered delicious. It was just that each country had its chocolate preferences. The Swiss liked it rich and milky, as did the British. The Italians liked it mixed with fruits and nuts. The Germans liked it dark and almost devoid of milk, often with hazelnuts. The Austrians blended it into pastries and filled it with flavored cream. The Dutch liked it light.

An enterprising young American named Milton Snavely Hershey saw the enormous popularity of milk chocolate in Europe. Like other businessmen before him, he decided that milk chocolate was the future for his family business. But Hershey dreamed bigger than most people. He saw chocolate as the future of an entire city, created by him and built entirely on the business of manufacturing chocolate.

Milton S. Hershey.

Hershey was born in 1857 in Lancaster County, Pennsylvania. He wasn't there long, however. Hershey's father moved the family frequently, drifting from one job to another. This made settling down difficult, and Milton was unable to attend school on a regular basis. For long periods of time, his father lived apart from the family while he was seeking work.

Traveling from place to place in the mid-1800s, young Milton was exposed to many different kinds of candy and decided he wanted to be a candy maker. He apprenticed with a confectioner as a teenager, and at the age of eighteen started his own caramel company in Philadelphia. At the time, caramels were one of the most popular types of candy. They were relatively easy to make, requiring little more than sugar, butter, vanilla, paraffin (a kind of edible wax), and a place to cook them at precise temperatures.

Despite his best efforts, Hershey couldn't make a success of the caramel business. There was just too much competition from people starting their own candy shops. He tried opening stores in other cities, but they failed as well. When he ran out of money, he went to live with his father, who had become a miner in Colorado. While there, he worked for a Denver candy maker who used fresh milk in his caramels instead of paraffin. Paraffin was used to make caramels chewy, but the milk made them even chewier.

Impressed with the flavor, and wanting to give the business another try, Hershey moved back to Pennsylvania. In 1886 he started the Lancaster Caramel Company. He made caramels as he'd learned out west—and this time his recipe was a huge success. A British company offered to sell them overseas, and Hershey's caramels became an international sensation. By the early 1890s he was one of the biggest caramel manufacturers anywhere.

In 1893, Hershey went to the Columbian Exposition in Chicago, a huge event that featured products, food, inventions, and music from countries all over the world. He was looking for some new candy ideas, and found them in a German company that was showing off its milk chocolate. Hershey fell in love with milk chocolate right then and there and was sure that it was the future of candy. He bought all the equipment that the German company had brought to the fair and sent it back to his factory in Pennsylvania. He was not, however, able to obtain their recipe for making milk chocolate.

Initially Hershey used the machines for simple chocolate products, like cocoa powder for baking and the coatings for his company's caramels. It was a kind of chocolate not much different from what the Frys had come up with decades before. And it wasn't unique: several American companies were already selling basic unsweetened chocolate.

There was Baker's Chocolate, established in the late 1700s, the oldest cocoa company in the United States. There was also the Ghirardelli Chocolate Company, one of the biggest businesses in the fast-growing state of California. The company was founded in 1852 by Domingo Ghirardelli, who had learned chocolate making in his hometown of Rapallo, Italy. Like thousands of others, he had moved to California during the gold rush of '49, hoping to strike it rich.

Ghirardelli didn't find any gold in California. Needing some type of income, he set up a small store. He sold equipment and food to other gold seekers . . . along with his own candy confections. By the time the gold rush had faded, Ghirardelli had established a thriving business in San Francisco selling chocolate and coffee.

In yet another path in the evolution of chocolate, one of Ghirardelli's employees accidentally discovered how to separate cocoa butter from cocoa mass without needing Van Houten's press. After hanging a bag of cocoa mass in a bag in a hot warehouse room, the employee later found that the temperature had caused the cocoa butter to seep out of the mass and drip through

Above: Ghirardelli advertised his chocolate products directly to California miners.

Right: Before he sold milk chocolate candy bars, Milton Hershey sold novelty products like "chocolate tablets."

the bag, leaving just the cocoa solids—the cocoa cake—in the bag. Ghirardelli saw that this somehow removed even more of the cocoa's natural bitterness than Van Houten's process and didn't require the addition of alkali salts. Ghirardelli chocolate became a phenomenon throughout California.

In addition to selling cocoa and cocoa powder, Ghirardelli began producing his own chocolate candies. His sons joined the company to help him expand. Their factory soon occupied a large section of San Francisco near Fisherman's Wharf, which came to be known as Ghirardelli Square. By 1893, when Hershey got into the chocolate business, the Ghirardelli family was already importing more than half a million pounds of cocoa beans a year.

But Milton Hershey had two things going for him: manufacturing and distribution. He had a large caramel factory in which to make candy, and he operated in a part of the country that was much more densely populated than

In 1898, Hershey's logo was the "Cocoa Bean Baby."

California. New York, Philadelphia, Baltimore, and Washington, D.C., were all just a few hours from his headquarters. Within seven years, Hershey was one of America's biggest chocolate producers, so big that he could sell his extra chocolate to other chocolate companies for use in their products.

To Hershey's mind, this success was marvelous but masked a big problem. He was producing chocolate, but he wasn't producing *milk* chocolate, the type of chocolate he steadfastly believed would change the chocolate industry. Hershey wasn't making milk chocolate for one simple reason: he didn't know how. Nobody in America did.

The secret recipes for milk chocolate were locked away in the vaults of the companies that owned them in Europe. Recipes were what made one brand of milk chocolate taste different from another, and they were guarded as important corporate secrets. In addition, no one had yet figured out Rodolphe Lindt's conching process. As an American interested in making milk chocolate, Milton Hershey was starting from scratch.

Hershey was ready to bet everything on milk chocolate becoming the candy of the future. He sold the Lancaster Caramel Company in 1900 for $1 million—an incredible sum at the time. He kept the growing chocolate side of the business for himself and set up a new factory near the town of Derry, Pennsylvania.

Even though he had just become a very rich man who could have retired and never worked again, Hershey devoted his days to figuring out how to make milk chocolate. At first, he didn't think it would be that difficult. After all, he knew a lot about making candies with milk. It was milk that had made his caramels so popular. And he'd learned a great deal about cocoa products, as well.

But like Daniel Peter and Rodolphe Lindt, Hershey struggled to find a way to make raw milk blend perfectly with cocoa butter and powder. He had plenty of milk at his disposal—like Switzerland and England, Pennsylvania was cow country—but he couldn't determine the right combination.

His experiments resulted in one formula that allowed him to make milk chocolate candy, but he couldn't produce it to taste the same in every batch. And it wasn't smooth and didn't have the melt-in-your-mouth quality that Swiss milk chocolate had. Nonetheless, he introduced these chocolates to the market in 1900—soon after he'd sold the caramel company—and they sold very well. They were the first Hershey's bars, but Milton wasn't satisfied with the product and kept working at finding a recipe that would produce consistently light and smooth milk chocolate by the ton, day in and day out.

One of Hershey's biggest issues was the same one that had plagued Daniel Peter: he couldn't get rid of all the water from his milk while he was mixing it with cocoa butter and cocoa powder. It really was a chemistry puzzle, and even the littlest change to each step would produce an entirely different chocolate.

Sometime around 1903 the day finally came when Hershey figured out how to make real milk chocolate. Like many stories from a hundred or more years ago, this one is missing quite a few important details. One version of the story has Hershey employing a German chemist to figure out the right way to treat the milk. The chemist worked for weeks but couldn't improve the chocolate, so Hershey fired him. After the chemist failed, a boiler operator from the old Lancaster Caramel Company stopped by the new factory and suggested a method he thought might work. It took the operator just two hours to get the process up and running. When he was done, the milk chocolate came out exactly as Hershey had wanted.

Another version of the story states that Hershey was using every single kind of milk product he could think of. He allegedly purchased a shipment of milk powder from Europe, but it had already begun spoiling. Not wanting to waste anything, he used the milk anyway. He mixed it in with his regular batches . . . and it worked.

Regardless of how it happened, Hershey had finally discovered a milk chocolate formula he was happy with. It had the same texture as Swiss milk chocolate, although it tasted a trifle sour. No matter; it was his own creation. And he was determined to make it something that every American, no matter how rich or poor, could enjoy.

His new and improved "sweet milk chocolate" bar was a solid rectangle of rich brown, with a wrapper that announced it as being a "Hershey's" bar. For many Americans, most of whom had never tasted milk chocolate, let alone knew what it was, this Hershey's bar was soon to become their favorite sweet.

Orders poured in immediately. In order to make his goal of chocolate for everyone a reality, Hershey set about building the world's biggest chocolate factory. The factory would produce so much chocolate that it would cost very little for people to buy. He stayed in Pennsylvania, in no small part because of its huge number of dairy farms. The Hershey process for creating milk chocolate—indeed, every recipe for milk chocolate—required huge amounts of fresh milk every day.

The factory wasn't all Hershey wanted to build. He wanted to create a town where everyone would work making chocolate, where the chocolate factory would employ anyone who wanted a job, where the chocolate company would build schools and a hospital, where the company would build the roads and operate a trolley, and where there would be parks and entertainment for everyone to enjoy—all provided by Hershey and his company.

In one of the more unusual slogans ever given to a candy bar, Hershey compared the nutritional value of his milk chocolate to meat.

Part of his motivation came from his upbringing. His mother had taught him that people should share their good fortune. And following his roaming father for years made Hershey long for a stable place to live and learn, where everyone had the opportunity to succeed.

Milton and his wife, Kitty, could not have children of their own. With their vast wealth, though, they wanted to make sure underpriviledged kids had a chance to have enjoyable childhoods. In their new town, they created an

orphanage and a school for children from broken homes. They visited those kids and threw parties for them and gave them everything they would have wished for their own children.

Above: Life in the town of Hershey centered around the original chocolate factory.

Right: The Hershey company held regular social events like picnics for its employees.

As the factory went up, Hershey hired architects and planners to build his town. People were moving to the middle of Pennsylvania to live in a town where there were free concerts every day, where an amusement park with roller coasters was being built, where golf courses and swimming pools were all just a short walk from the homes built by the Hershey Chocolate Company. The town had no name, because it wasn't technically a town: it was a large tract of land owned by Hershey. But since Milton Hershey served as everything from mayor to fire chief, it was simply called Hershey, Pennsylvania.

Sale of his chocolate bars succeeded beyond anyone's wildest dreams. In 1908 Hershey created a second milk chocolate bar by adding almonds. These two candy bars were the main "bar" offering from the Hershey Chocolate Company, and they have remained so up to this day. But it was a little dollop of milk chocolate that would make Hershey the most popular candy maker in the United States.

In 1907, the company introduced little foil-wrapped pieces of chocolate that it called Kisses. The candy was created by a machine that dropped "tears" of chocolate onto a flat mold. The sound that the machine made each time it formed a chocolate resembled a loud kiss, so Hershey decided to use that as the name. (That's one story; there were actually sugar candies at the time called kisses, which were often given as romantic gifts.)

Each teardrop-shaped chocolate—with a flat bottom from hitting the mold—was foil wrapped by hand. Its milk chocolate richness and one-bite size made it an immediate favorite across America. Even though the Hershey's bar was what drew buyers to Hershey's milk chocolate, the Hershey's Kiss became—and remains—one of the most recognizable candies ever created. Chocolate can be molded into many forms, but nothing before or since has had as distinctive a shape as the Hershey's Kiss.

Hershey's Kiss is one of the most recognizable candies in the world. It was invented over one hundred years ago.

With these three products, Milton Hershey introduced America to milk chocolate and made it cheap enough that everyone could afford it. Hershey's bars were just a nickel and stayed at that price until 1969 (that year, the price was doubled to a dime). Even schoolkids with a little bit of pocket change could buy a bar.

Hershey was the first person to mass-produce chocolate on a scale that allowed him to ship chocolate every day to every part of the United States. Two things, both of his own creation, helped him with this.

The first was the mixture he used to make his milk chocolate. Milk chocolate melts more quickly than basic (unsweetened or non-milk) chocolate. Basic chocolate has a melting point of about 90 degrees Fahrenheit, but milk chocolate starts to get soft at temperatures around 75 degrees Fahrenheit and becomes almost liquid above 90 degrees Fahrenheit. (You know this if you've ever carried a bar around in your pocket for more than a few minutes, or held a piece in your hand. It becomes a fluid mess.)

This temperature problem explains why many large chocolate makers couldn't ship milk chocolate to other countries. It wouldn't last the journey in solid pieces, or it would spoil. It also explains why so many milk chocolatiers were located in northern regions of the United States, like Pennsylvania, New York, New England, and Illinois, as well as in some of the colder European countries, like England, Switzerland, and Germany. During hot summer months, many chocolate makers would have to stop production or risk having entire batches melt—this was before the invention of air-conditioning.

Something in Hershey's formula—which is still a closely guarded secret— kept the milk chocolate from melting or spoiling as quickly as his competitors' bars. In addition, Hershey wrapped his chocolate in heavy paper or foil to protect it. Most candy at the turn of the century was sold in bulk and wasn't wrapped. Treats like licorice or sour balls were displayed in big glass cases or containers, and customers picked them out one piece at a time. They had no idea who the original manufacturer was—in some cases, the candy was made in the store itself. Hershey's wrapper not only protected his chocolate, it told

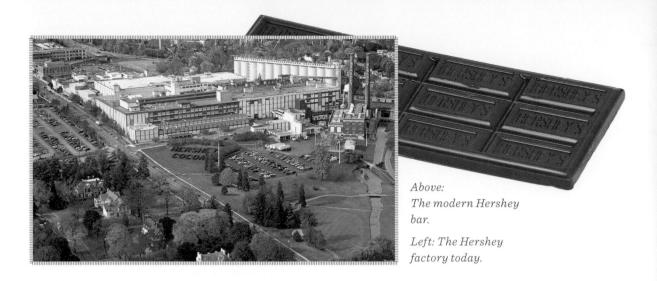

Above:
The modern Hershey bar.

Left: The Hershey factory today.

every buyer that it was made by Hershey. One story claims that Milton never viewed his discarded wrappers as garbage or litter—he considered them advertising. In America the name Hershey became synonymous with chocolate.

In addition to introducing America to the joys of chocolate, Hershey had made his dream of creating a real town based on chocolate come to fruition. People moved from all over the country to live and work in Hershey, Pennsylvania. Not only that, the town and the factory became a tourist attraction. With its Hersheypark amusement park, streetlights shaped like Kisses, streets named Cocoa Avenue and Chocolate Avenue—not to mention the fantastic smell of chocolate that filled the air—the town Hershey created was unlike any other place in America. So many people flocked to Hershey that Milton built a hotel and restaurants to take care of visitors.

By the time World War I broke out in 1914, the Hershey Chocolate Company was so big that it was selling excess chocolate to smaller competitors as well as to bakeries. For example, Hershey's cocoa powder was purchased by the National Biscuit Company (known today as Nabisco) to flavor its Oreo cookies. Despite numerous efforts by competitors, the hearts, minds, mouths, and wallets of chocolate lovers were Hershey's. No one else came close.

That wouldn't change until after the war, when a man from Minneapolis—and the son he had abandoned—would take on the entire world of chocolate. And they would win.

THE CANDY BATTLES

WHEN THE UNITED STATES ENTERED WORLD War I in 1917, it sent over a million soldiers to Europe to fight. These troops had to be fed every day, and many of them had to be fed out on the battlefields, far from kitchens and a ready supply of fresh food. So they were provided with portable rations, foods they could carry with them. The food had to be nourishing. This meant things like canned sardines and canned corned beef as well as hard biscuits and crackers. And, unlike in previous wars, something else was added: packaged chocolate. The commanders in

American troops in France during World War I.

charge of the troops viewed chocolate not only as a quick source of nourishment and sugar but also as a treat that would keep the soldiers' spirits up.

Given its packaging, the Hershey's bar became the preferred chocolate for military food kits, although products from Baker's Chocolate, Hershey's long-time competitor in New England, were also used. Seemingly overnight, hundreds of thousands of U.S. troops were getting a regular supply of Hershey's bars—and getting used to eating them. Its popularity in the military made Hershey the first candy brand to be recognized nationwide.

There were thousands of small confectioners across America making candy with chocolate, but no single brand that everyone knew. Every region—indeed, every big city—had its own candy makers using their recipes to make unique candy. But because these candy makers weren't large enough to make their own milk chocolate (or afford too much of it), much of their candy was a blend of chocolate with nuts, or candied fruit, or molasses, or caramel, or something called nougat, which was a chewy blend of eggs, corn syrup, and sugar.

The Standard Candy Company of Nashville had a local favorite with its Goo Goo Cluster, a soft patty of marshmallow nougat and peanuts coated in chocolate that it had created in 1912. Chicago's Williamson Company made a bar that featured a blend of peanuts, caramel, and fudge all dipped in chocolate that it called the Oh Henry!, in honor of a handsome young man named Henry who was fawned over by the company's female employees. The Whitmans, a Philadelphia family, sold little tin boxes of their signature chocolate-dipped confections, called samplers. (During World War I, the Whitmans packaged these tins with tiny versions of popular books, and sent them off to the troops.)

Perhaps most famously, as far back as 1896, Leo Hirschfield of Brooklyn had made penny candies that were individually wrapped to keep them clean—making him one of the first to wrap any sweets. The most popular of his offerings was a tiny caramel flavored with chocolate that he named after his daughter, whose nickname was Tootsie. The resulting "Tootsie Roll" was, in every sense of the word, a sensation.

When World War I was over in 1918, American soldiers returned home and started buying their own Hershey's bars. Demand for milk chocolate in all forms skyrocketed, thanks largely to Hershey's products. It also helped that

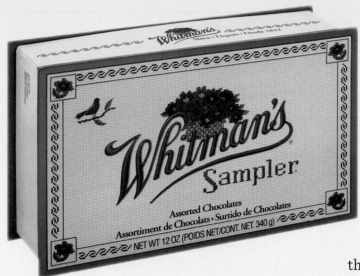

The Whitman's Sampler box of chocolates has been part of American culture for nearly one hundred years.

many smaller candy makers had begun to develop their own recipes for milk chocolate.

Making large batches of milk chocolate was still an expensive undertaking, due to the cost of raw cocoa beans. Only U.S. companies as large as Hershey or Baker's, or Nestlé and Cadbury in Europe, could afford to mass-produce milk chocolate and keep costs low. But because they were so large, they could pass on some savings to their customers who were buying chocolate to make their own products. As we've seen, these smaller manufacturers' candies were usually mixed with inexpensive ingredients like nuts and almonds or nougat and caramel. That way, they could still make a good-size "chocolate candy" while keeping the cost down by using less chocolate.

Supplying these smaller companies was a decent business for Hershey, since they covered their little candies with Hershey's milk chocolate or flavored them with Hershey's cocoa powder. Hershey's biggest client by far was a man named Frank Mars, who ran a small Minneapolis confectionery company called Mar-O-Bar.

Frank Mars was a candy maker in the classical sense of making sugar sweets—he was not a chocolate man. Born in Minnesota in 1882, Mars had been stricken with polio shortly after birth, and never had the full use of his legs. Not able to participate in sports or even go for walks, he sat

Frank Mars, the founder of Mars, Inc.

for hours every day in the kitchen with his mother. She was a good and prolific cook and gave Frank projects to keep him occupied. One of these was making sugar candies, ranging from caramels to hard crystal treats.

At age nineteen, when he was old enough to move out on his own, Frank tried to start his own candy business. He married a woman named Ethel, and they made hard sugar candies such as peppermint sticks to sell to candy shops and drugstores. Frank went on the road to sell his products, but the competition was fierce, and there were better candies out there. Mars spent weeks at a time away from his wife and their son, Forrest, calling on stores across the Midwest. He frequently had a problem with spoilage—his candy would go bad because it took him so long to sell it.

Ultimately, his business failed, and Frank had no money—for anything. Unable to pay rent or buy groceries, Ethel M. Mars divorced Frank in 1908, and took six-year-old Forrest away to live with her parents. Frank would not see Forrest for another fifteen years.

Peppermint sticks were popular with candy makers in the early 1900s because they were easy to produce and had inexpensive ingredients.

Frank continued to make and sell candy, unsuccessfully, for years—until he came upon an unusual recipe for butter creams, semisoft candies made of sugar, butter, cream, and vanilla. Like Milton Hershey with his discovery of a great caramel recipe, Frank Mars suddenly had a candy everyone wanted. His butter creams became one of the most popular treats available in the Midwest.

Mars's fortunes turned around dramatically. He married another woman, also named Ethel, opened a small factory, and took an interest in raising and racing horses. He tried to do something unique with milk chocolate, but his ideas—usually some confection or other dipped in milk chocolate—were not exciting enough to get people to choose Mars's chocolates over the competition. Butter creams, and not chocolate, were making money for Frank Mars.

In 1923, the now twenty-one-year-old Forrest Mars was a salesman for a cigarette company. He had the novel idea of hanging advertising posters for the cigarettes over the windows of Chicago department stores. This happened to be illegal. Forrest was arrested, and while he was in jail, a man who was in town on a business trip bailed him out. That man was his father. Frank had read about his son's arrest in the local paper and showed up to help him.

It was the first time the two had seen each other since Forrest was six.

Frank took Forrest back to Minneapolis with him, and it was immediately clear that the two were not destined to get along. Frank's business was moderately successful, but it did almost all of its business in Minnesota and the surrounding states. His candies couldn't be shipped long distances, and because of his new family and racing interests, he was no longer willing to travel far to make sales calls. Forrest scoffed at these excuses, blaming his father's inability to grow his business on not being able to come up with exciting products. They were arguing about it over lunch one day, and Frank—quite fed up with his son—asked him what *he* would do. Forrest taunted his father by pointing to his milkshake and saying, "Why don't you put this chocolate malted drink into a candy bar?"

Soon afterward, Forrest left to go to college in California. Frank took his son's suggestion to heart—although he later claimed it was his own idea—and created a chewy chocolate-malt-flavored nougat. He placed some caramel over it and then dipped the whole thing in chocolate. The thin milk chocolate coating solidified around the unusual nougat inside, making it a superb blend of different tastes and textures. As an unforeseen benefit, the chocolate helped protect the nougat from spoiling. Frank called it the Milky Way bar and introduced it in 1924.

A heated discussion with his son had been the inspiration for a formula that would make Frank Mars's family the richest in America.

Even though chocolate bars were all the rage, it was the malt-flavored nougat that made Mars's candy unique. Frank focused on that part of his bar, opting to buy his chocolate for the coating from somewhere else. The Mar-O-Bar company was not huge by national standards, and even though the Milky Way was gaining popularity outside of the Midwest, its operations were relatively small.

To meet the demand for his new bar, Frank needed a chocolate supplier who would allow him to buy the chocolate on credit. That meant he would pay the supplier as soon as he was paid for his Milky Ways. The supplier would have to trust that he would be able to pay in the future. Given his former business failures, most suppliers refused to do business with him. All except the Hershey Chocolate Company, which agreed to take a chance on Frank Mars.

Mars was grateful to the Hershey Chocolate Company, and especially to William Murrie, the man who had taken over day-to-day operations as Milton Hershey got older and spent more time developing his town and attending to the needs of the orphanage and school. Mars became Hershey's most loyal, and biggest, customer. Murrie saw that Mars had developed a whole new type of candy bar with his nougat-based Milky Way—and it didn't compete directly with the solid chocolate success of the Hershey's Milk Chocolate bar and Hershey's Kiss. Murrie and Mars came to view each other as not only successful business partners but as friends.

The popularity of the Milky Way bar also inspired Frank Mars to move his company, which he had renamed Mars, Incorporated. He needed to be based in a bigger city than Minneapolis that had lots of railroad and highway traffic for better distribution around the country. That city was Chicago.

Despite the presence of Hershey in Pennsylvania and the scores of confectioners in East Coast cities like New York, Boston, and Philadelphia, Chicago was the candy center of America in the early 1900s. There were a number of reasons why. Chicago's weather was rarely too hot, which meant that candy could be produced all year round. It was located in the heart of the Midwest, and milk products were readily available from nearby dairy farms. It had one of the best railroad hubs in the United States, serving as a central point for freight

A magazine advertisement describing the new Milky Way bar.

traveling cross-country. It had modern buildings and factories, many of which had been recently constructed in the aftermath of the Great Chicago Fire of 1871. Candy makers could find everything they needed in and around Chicago, from ingredients to shipping.

One of the first people to put Chicago on the national candy map was Otto Schnering. Born in Chicago in 1891, Schnering attended the University of Chicago and then found work as a piano salesman. When the piano company went out of business, Schnering was out of a job. He did have money saved up, though. He heard about candy-making equipment that was selling for one hundred dollars and decided to try his hand at making his own. After all, it was 1916, and people all over the country were becoming successful making candy. Just look at Milton Hershey.

Schnering set up shop in the vacant back room of a local hardware store. He called his new business the Curtiss Candy Company, in honor of his mother's maiden name. Like nearly every fledgling candy maker in America, Schnering tried his hand at the penny candy basics, from sour balls to mints. They weren't much different from any of the myriad other candies offered in Chicago, and they didn't sell well.

One thing Schnering discovered very quickly was that almost every candy lover liked peanuts, caramel, or chocolate. So he decided that he would put them all together in a single candy. He made a bar that featured a blend of roasted peanuts and caramel, and then dipped the whole thing in chocolate. He called it the Kandy Kake, even though there was nothing cakelike about it. But it gave his confection an unusual name—Schnering liked unusual names—and set it apart from most of the other bars in Chicago.

Working tirelessly, Schnering went door to door with his new candy. In the course of three weeks, he convinced 249 stores in downtown Chicago to carry at least one Kandy Kake bar. According to company legend, new orders for more Kandy Kakes started coming in the morning after his first delivery. A chocolate success was born.

At least temporarily. Within the year, Curtiss had more competition, including people copying his bar. It was getting harder to stand out from the crowd. He decided to take drastic measures.

The first was to lower the price of the Kandy Kake. Ever since he'd set up shop, Schnering had used large industrial machines to produce his candy, while most confectioners were still doing everything by hand or with small kitchen machines. He knew he could drop his price and still make more money per piece than his competitors, because he had fewer people to pay. He decided to charge a nickel for his bar. The next thing he did, in 1921, was change the name. He wanted something catchy, something that everyone would remember. He came up with the name Baby Ruth.

There are two very different stories about how he chose Baby Ruth. Schnering said throughout his life that he named it after "Baby" Ruth Cleveland, the young daughter of President Grover Cleveland. She had been born in 1891, between her father's two terms as U.S president, and died at the age of twelve. She was the subject of many magazine and newspaper articles during her short life

The Curtiss Candy company promoted Baby Ruth as a magical and nutritious treat.

and fascinated the American public in the way that all children of presidents have done. Plus, she had been born just six days before Schnering himself back in 1891. Schnering claimed the name was a tribute to the young celebrity who had died seventeen years earlier.

A lovely story, but many of Schnering's associates disputed it. They claimed that the Baby Ruth, as many people suspected, was named after baseball icon Babe Ruth. According to them, the star baseball player was as famous as any athlete in America, and Schnering had approached Babe Ruth about using his name for the repackaged Kandy Kake bar. Ruth wanted an exorbitant amount of money from the Curtiss company, and Schnering wouldn't pay it. Instead, he changed "Babe" to "Baby," and concocted the neat story about celebrating little Ruth Cleveland.

The truth? No one knows—but the second one seems more likely. Babe Ruth had just hit fifty-four home runs for the New York Yankees and was considered the greatest living baseball player. His exploits were in the papers almost every day. Everyone knew who he was. Ruth Cleveland had died in 1904, and had been out of the public's mind for years.

Schnering stuck to his story so strongly that when Babe Ruth tried to start his own candy line—using his name—Curtiss sued to stop him, saying the name was too close to "Baby Ruth." In an ironic twist, Curtiss won.

Whatever the real story, the Baby Ruth bar was one of the first non-solid chocolate bar successes anywhere. (It predated the Milky Way by three years.) Schnering followed it up several years later with one of the first crunchy chocolate bars ever made. It had a flaky and crispy center—made of a secret combination of peanut butter and caramel—that was then dipped in chocolate. Instead of naming the new bar himself, he held a contest to come up with a new and unusual name. The winning entry was "Butterfinger."

Schnering was dubbed the Candy Bar King. As Milton Hershey had done in Pennsylvania, he ended up buying land outside of Chicago that grew to become a sort of company town where he produced candy and had a dairy farm. His employees were provided with free chicken, milk, and eggs, and he paid for some of the public services in town and hosted its parades. The Curtiss company also gave free candy to charity events in and around Chicago.

Even with all of his success, Schnering didn't remain Chicago's leading chocolate bar manufacturer for long. That's because in 1929 Frank Mars moved his entire company, including two hundred employees, from Minnesota to the Chicago suburbs.

Frank spent lavishly to create a palace dedicated to candy. To passersby, the new Mars factory looked like a mansion or a grand resort. Inside, Frank had it decorated with fine art and stained-glass windows. He made sure he had the finest equipment money could buy. His company was growing so quickly that Frank Mars had more money than he had ever imagined—or than he knew what to do with. He bought a company airplane and a horse farm in Tennessee that he named Milky Way Farm.

THE HOME OF MILKY WAY CONFECTIONS

You naturally would expect unusually fine candies such as MILKY WAY CONFECTIONS to be made under the finest conditions possible. In these spotless kitchens, you find everyone in snowy white uniforms and caps. Fresh air and sunshine in abundance. No wonder MILKY WAY CONFECTIONS taste so good...are so pure and wholesome. The finest quality ingredients blended by the most skillful workers in the most modern institution of its kind.

Mars was so proud of its headquarters and factories that it featured them on boxes of chocolates.

The year before, Forrest had graduated from college. He was a smart guy, having attended both Berkeley and Yale, so—despite their disagreements—his father hired him to come work at the Chicago factory and learn the business. But although he was extremely intelligent, Forrest was by all accounts an abrasive and confrontational person. He alienated many of the workers who had been with the company for years—and knew far more about candy than he did.

For a while, Frank chose not to deal with the turmoil Forrest was causing. He was too busy introducing new variations of his chocolate-coated nougat bars. The first, in 1930, was called Snickers. It was the same basic construction as a Milky Way, except that it had nuts atop the caramel and nougat.

Above right: Snickers Bars were named after the prized family horse.

Below: A nickel used to buy three 3 Musketeers bars.

And the name? It came from his wife's favorite horse, which was named Snickers. Two years later, Frank came up with the 3 Musketeers bar, which was basically the chocolate-coated nougat without anything added to it. The bar got its name because it originally was made up of three smaller bars—each a different nougat flavor—packaged together: chocolate, vanilla, and strawberry. The strawberry and vanilla flavors were soon dropped, but the name was not.

All of these bars were huge successes, and soon Mars was the second largest producer of chocolate candy in the United States—right behind Hershey. That was good enough for Frank but not for Forrest. He prodded his father to start selling their products internationally, which Frank had no interest in doing. Forrest was relentless, and his attitude, coupled with the dislike many employees had for him, pushed Frank to his limit.

He fired his own son from Mars, Inc. in 1932, and gave him $50,000 to go away and do something on his own. Forrest immediately moved to Europe, intent on learning how the chocolate business was handled on the other side of the Atlantic.

In 1934, Frank Mars died at age fifty, leaving his company in the hands of his wife and daughter. Forrest didn't bother to go back to America for the funeral.

Europe had been enjoying milk chocolate since Daniel Peter and Rodolphe Lindt each unveiled their candy creations to the world. Yet the European regional makers faced the exact same problems that plagued their American counterparts: distance and weather prevented them from selling outside their own countries or geographic regions. This meant that to the English, "chocolate" tasted like Cadbury's, to the Swiss it was Lindt and Peter-Cailler, to the Italians it was Perugina, and on and on. And each country was very protective of its brands.

There were some standouts and new additions among the regional manufacturers. In 1905, the Cadbury company had developed its own milk chocolate bar for the British market, featuring more whole milk than any bar created in Europe or America. It was called the Dairy Milk bar and was advertised as containing a glass and a half of milk in every bar. Obviously, most of the water in the milk was evaporated during manufacturing, but Cadbury's claim gives an indication how much milk was needed to produce even a small amount of milk chocolate. It was creamier and had a fuller texture than the bars Milton Hershey was producing. Soon the Dairy Milk was the most popular bar by far in England, which was quite an accomplishment in a country that had hundreds of chocolate makers.

Cadbury wanted customers to know that its chocolate contained more milk than its competitors.

Theodor Tobler, a young man whose father owned a chocolate shop in Bern, Switzerland, developed his own brand of milk chocolate candy in 1908. Working with a cousin, he mixed crushed nuts and nougat together and then immersed

Theodor Tobler designed his chocolate bar to resemble pyramids. Do you see the standing bear, a reference to the Bern coat of arms, hidden in the image of the mountain?

them in chocolate, creating a lightly crunchy candy. To further distinguish his bars from the numerous milk chocolates coming to market, he shaped them like miniature pyramids or triangles instead of flat rectangles. He was said to have been inspired by the Swiss Alp mountains as well as the human pyramids he saw created by local dance troupes. Regardless of its origin, the unique taste and shape quickly set Tobler's chocolate—which he called Toblerone—apart from everything else in Europe.

Brothers Henry and Joseph Rowntree of York, England, created something entirely novel in the 1930s by dipping very thin and crisp layers of sugar cookies in chocolate. Their invention would eventually be called Kit Kat, after a popular club where politicians gathered.

The end of World War I had helped break many chocolate makers out of their regional isolation. New factories of all sorts were built after 1918, and those factories featured brand-new machines and technologies. For the first time, European chocolate makers could mass-produce candy bars on the same scale as Milton Hershey. Improvements in shipping, and in keeping products cool, allowed regional chocolate makers to start selling all across Europe.

As chocolate companies got bigger, they started gobbling up their competitors. John Cadbury's family purchased its longtime foe J. S. Fry in 1919,

THE CANDY BATTLES

73

immediately after the war, and began shipping its chocolates across the English Channel. The Peter-Cailler company merged with Charles-Amédée Kohler's business; Kohler was the man who had taught Rodolphe Lindt how to make chocolate. The combined company, Peter, Cailler, Kohler, was bought by Nestlé in 1929. By the time that happened, both Daniel Peter and Henri Nestlé were dead, so neither man saw the companies that bore their names join together. In an odd twist, when the Nestlé company bought Peter, Cailler, Kohler, it marked the first time that Nestlé—despite its tradition of developing milk products—had sold milk chocolate. The names of the men who helped make edible chocolate a reality lived on, even if the men themselves did not.

It was into this competitive world that Forrest Mars inserted himself. He got low-level jobs working at the Nestlé chocolate factory and then at the Tobler factory. Neither company knew Forrest was a member of the Mars candy family. As he worked, he observed every stage of production, taking measurements of ingredients and the time spent on each process, and getting as close to figuring out their milk chocolate recipes as he could. After a year of this "industrial spying," Forrest went to England to start his own chocolate business.

He took the formula for the Milky Way bar and set about making a candy that the British would enjoy. He made it sweeter than its American version by adding more caramel and covered it with milk chocolate he purchased from Cadbury's. And, so no one would confuse his candy bar with the one produced by his father's company in America, Forrest called it simply the Mars bar. It didn't take long for shops around London to start carrying it.

One thing that Forrest had learned in America was that size matters. For example, the Hershey's bar was a flat rectangle that cost a nickel. But the Milky Way and Snickers bars were thick and plump and also cost a nickel. Granted, the Milky Way and Snickers weren't made solely of milk chocolate, but when it came to figuring out how much you could get for a nickel, size could sway buyers toward the nougat-filled candies.

The same thing was true in England. Forrest was going up against Cadbury's Dairy Milk bar—a flat rectangle, like the Hershey's bar—and offerings from the Rowntree brothers. When he put his much thicker Mars bar on the shelf next to the competition, he started getting sales. Word spread across the English Channel, to places like Belgium and France, about this inexpensive milk chocolate candy that had an unusual center. Forrest was able to do what his father had never been interested in doing—sell his candy internationally.

This was a huge feat. Most regions of Europe were very particular and protective about their milk chocolate, usually shunning foreign imports as inferior. The Hershey's bar is the best example of this. While many Americans think of Hershey's as the quintessential chocolate bar—it dominates holidays like Halloween and advertises itself as "The Great American Chocolate Bar"—Europeans and the British disdain the Hershey's bar. Most of them will not eat it.

There's actually a good reason for this dislike. The Hershey's bar has a distinctly sour smell when compared to European chocolates. This is due to the original formula devised by Milton Hershey in 1903—the alleged "spoiled powder"—which has changed very little in the past hundred years.

Forrest Mars knew that bigger was better when it came to buying candy bars.

You can test this for yourself: take a plain chocolate bar that has its origins overseas, like the Cadbury Dairy Milk bar, and smell it. It has a huge cocoa aroma. Then do the same thing with a Hershey's bar (it has to be a Hershey's bar, because some other Hershey products use a different chocolate formula). When you smell it, there's something completely different in its aroma—less like cocoa and more like cheese. The same is true of the taste. For Europeans used to a richer chocolate flavor, the Hershey's bar doesn't compare, and they won't buy it. Many of them refer to it as "barnyard chocolate."

The Mars bar had three different flavors designed to appeal to a wide audience.

The Mars bar was the first chocolate bar to appeal to a wide variety of international tastes, but it was also where Forrest's candy bar success began and ended. Like his father's chocolates, the Mars bar's appeal was built on nougat. Forrest couldn't get any of his other candy ideas to take off. Not that it mattered much to him. Forrest was interested in exploring lots of ideas—regardless of where they came from—and hoping to get rich off all of them.

One area where he saw a growing market, completely unrelated to chocolate, was pet food. Most people in England and Europe fed their dogs and cats leftovers or kitchen scraps. He came across a small company selling canned meat for pets and decided he could promote it on the premise that it was better for animals than scraps. He purchased the company and, after aggressive advertising, had another winner on his hands. Soon Mars, Inc. was selling almost as much canned pet food as it was Mars bars.

By 1939, Mars was the third-largest confectionery company in England. Life was about to get very complicated for Forrest Mars, though. World War II was on the horizon. It would change his life, and the chocolate industry, very dramatically.

CHOCOLATE AND THE SECOND WORLD WAR

8

WORLD WAR II STARTED IN EUROPE IN 1939, TWO years before America got involved. European countries, including Britain, ramped up their military forces to try to stop the Nazis and to protect themselves. This required money: to pay soldiers, to outfit and feed them, to build tanks and planes, and to move it all to battlefields around the world. It also required resources that most people took for granted, including metals like copper and steel, cloth, sugar, coffee, and many other things that were needed to build machines and help the troops. Many of these products were diverted to the war effort, and they were provided only in limited amounts, or rations, to everyday citizens.

American soldiers in World War II were encouraged to share their chocolate rations with children in European towns.

One of the ways the British government sought to raise money was by placing a large tax on residents from other countries who worked in England. Forrest Mars was one of them. Despite his company being based in England, he was still an American citizen. Mars, for his part, wasn't interested in paying a tax that he thought was outrageous. Instead, he handed his company over to one of his English employees—temporarily—and returned to the United States.

But no one there welcomed him back. After the death of his father, his stepmother and half sister had taken control of Mars, Inc., and were now running it. They had no interest in having the family troublemaker join them in their candy business.

Forrest was too motivated a person to sit around and hope the war would end soon so he could go back to England. He needed to do something while he was in America. He knew the candy business, and he decided he would create a brand-new candy company, even if it competed with his relatives.

He had an idea for a new product, although the idea wasn't his. While traveling throughout Europe selling his Mars bars, he had come across Spanish soldiers eating small bead-like chocolates that were soft on the inside but hard on the outside. They actually cracked a little when you bit through their chocolate shell, creating a singular candy experience. And it seemed as if they never melted or spoiled—Forrest had even brought some with him to the United States. Weeks later, they still tasted good. The name of the Spanish candy maker who produced them has been lost to history.

Avoiding his own family, Forrest went to the Hershey Chocolate Company and met with its president, William Murrie. Milton Hershey was in ill health, and it was Murrie who now ran the business. He had been friends with Frank Mars and, unlike Forrest, had gone to Frank's funeral.

Forrest didn't want to talk about his father; he wanted to talk about a new business. He was eager to create his own version of the Spanish candy, and he wanted to start a new company to do it. He already had the money, and he had a factory lined up and ready to go. All he needed was someone to partner with, someone who could handle the chocolate side of the business. How about Murrie's son, Bruce?

Murrie, who was getting older and didn't know how much longer he would be at Hershey, liked the fact that he might be able to help his son in a new candy venture. And he was impressed with the candy itself. Bruce Murrie liked the idea, too, and agreed to be part of it. Forrest put up 80 percent of the costs to get the factory running, while the Murries put up the remaining 20 percent. The button-shaped treats were even named after Mars and Murrie's new partnership: M&M's Chocolate Candies.

Mars & Murrie would get its chocolate from

Above: William Murrie

Right: M&Ms were popular in World War II because they were easy to carry and didn't melt quickly.

Hershey, and would be a preferred Hershey customer. (There is much speculation that the only reason Mars took on Bruce Murrie was so he would have a direct link to the man who ran Hershey.) The first M&M's rolled off the factory line in 1940 and immediately became the newest chocolate fad in America. Only this fad didn't pass—it has continued growing to this day.

Just as M&M's were becoming a staple of stores across the country, the United States entered World War II. Immediately all types of goods and manufacturing plants were turned over to the war effort. Factories that once made cars and trucks were now making tanks. Industries that needed ingredients like sugar and coffee and cocoa were told that they would have to make do with less. These materials had to be used for soldiers' rations—and because of the war, it was going to be difficult even to get them in America. They were typically imported from other countries, and that was hard to do with ships getting attacked and ports being used to build and maintain warships. Americans in every state had to start scrimping and using less of these precious items.

One company that didn't have to scrimp was Hershey. William Murrie had made a deal with the U.S. military to be the primary provider of chocolate bars to the army. Not just any bar, but a special product known as Ration D. This was to be eaten by soldiers in times of emergency or when food was running out. Ration D was roughly twice as thick as a regular Hershey's bar, designed to handle higher-than-normal temperatures (many troops were going to the searing tropical heat of the South Pacific), and included flour to help keep it solid and make it more nutritious. By all accounts, the bar wasn't very tasty—it wasn't milk chocolate and didn't have much sugar—but it did the job of providing concentrated nutrition to soldiers.

Hershey's contract with the army meant that it could keep its factory open during wartime. As part of that agreement, nearly three-quarters of Hershey's chocolate production during World War II went straight to the military. Reportedly, at the war's peak, more than three million bars a day were being produced. In addition to the Ration D, which eventually became known as the Hershey's Tropical Chocolate Bar, regular Hershey's bars were included in the ration kits for troops headed to Europe. (Cadbury did the same for English and Australian troops.) American soldiers were encouraged to give the chocolate bars out to local citizens as symbols of friendship.

The only Hershey product that suffered was the Kiss. Because of the need for aluminum to build military equipment, Hershey could no longer get the distinctive foil it needed to wrap the little chocolates. Production of Kisses was halted until the war was over.

When it came to the actual chocolate business, though, Hershey's corporate customers were taken care of. Murrie made sure that Forrest Mars got as much chocolate as he needed to make M&M's. It helped M&M's fortunes that its hard-shelled, non-melting candy was a perfect chocolate to give to soldiers, no matter where they were stationed. Mars & Murrie soon had its own contract with the military, which helped keep the newly formed company afloat during wartime.

Another customer who got a steady supply of chocolate was a man named Harry Reese. He was a former Hershey employee and a friend of both William Murrie and Milton Hershey. Reese, known to everyone as H.B., had worked at Hershey as far back as 1917, having been employed on one of the company's dairy farms, and later in the factory shipping room. Seeing how quickly the Hershey Chocolate Company grew convinced him to try his hand at making chocolates. Reese had some ideas of his own and started working on them at home. There was something else behind his efforts other than just an urge to make chocolate, however: creating chocolates might bring in more money to help support his wife and sixteen children.

When H.B. perfected his recipes, which were quite good, he quit Hershey sometime in the early 1920s—on good terms—and started selling his confections in and around Derry. His candy was similar to what companies like Whitman's were making: flavored creams dipped in chocolate. Reese's

Harry Reese supported his large family by making chocolate cups filled with peanut butter.

flavors included coconut, caramel, marshmallow, peppermint, raisin, and peanut butter.

Since he wasn't making solid chocolate bars that would compete with their products, and he had been a good employee, Hershey and Murrie were happy to help H.B. out. They extended credit to Reese, and gave him free sugar when times were tough. When he set up a small factory in the town—employing many of his children—they even let him advertise his chocolates as being "manufactured in Hershey," a tagline that helped establish Reese's credibility.

When the war came, though, H.B. was hit like the other small candy makers in America. While he could get chocolate from Hershey, he couldn't get enough sugar to make all the caramel and coconut cream that he needed. One ingredient he did have plenty of—because it didn't require nearly as much sugar—was peanut butter. He switched his production to making what were called penny cups: little milk chocolate cups filled with peanut butter and topped with a layer of chocolate that sold for one cent each. Officially called Reese's Peanut Butter Cups, the candy had that one special element that resulted in successful chocolates: it was deliciously unlike anything else that customers could buy. And, at a penny, it was a good value and readily available during wartime.

The end of the war in 1945 saw huge changes in the chocolate world. While the Hershey Chocolate Company had succeeded in part by helping the military, smaller companies had been affected by the cocoa and sugar shortages and were struggling

Despite chocolate shortages, Reese's Peanut Butter Cups were sold throughout the course of World War II. But the price eventually doubled from a penny to two cents.

Milton Hershey sitting with students of his school in 1913.

to survive. The Mars and Murrie partnership was better off than most. It had produced a popular candy, but not as popular or profitable as Forrest wanted. What he really wanted was the company his father had built.

One person who didn't live to see the aftermath of the war was Milton Hershey. He died on October 13, 1945, only a few months after it ended. Hershey had lived alone in his last years, his wife having died years earlier. Never having had children of his own, he left all his money and most of the stock in his company to his cherished Hershey school and the orphanage. That meant everything the Hershey empire did from that day forward—from its candy business to its theme park to its hotel—would benefit the underprivileged children who went there.

Today the Milton Hershey School is the largest boarding school in the United States, providing free education and housing to more than a thousand kids, from pre-kindergarten through high school, who come from poor or broken homes. It is a complete education still funded, more than a hundred years later, by one man's idea of making a chocolate that every American could afford.

9

CORPORATIONS MADE OF CHOCOLATE

THE AFTERMATH OF THE WAR CHANGED THE business, but it really didn't change chocolate itself. The recipes for making popular chocolate bars were tried and true; the only hurdle was how to make more of them.

Postwar chocolate making was all about efficiency. Better factories, better shipping, better refrigeration, faster time from factory to store. It was also about big business. Companies of all sorts grew rapidly, from auto manufacturers and electronics companies to home builders, as millions of soldiers returned home. Regional companies joined together or were acquired by rivals to create ever larger companies that could compete on a national level. This was true in nearly every nation that had been affected by World War II.

26—The Modern Office Building of the Hershey Chocolate Corporation, Hershey, Pa.

The huge Hershey factory was an example of the growing demand for chocolate all over the world.

The chocolate industry was affected as much as any other business. In some ways, it was affected more. The chocolate business had been built by entrepreneurial men and their families who had toiled for years to make candies that would be scooped up by eager customers. They had, by and large, created their own formulas and perfected their own recipes in order to tempt the public.

Large companies bought smaller confectionery companies so they could offer more products to the stores that sold their products. These small companies were not in any position to compete with their larger brethren because they couldn't manufacture as cheaply, and they didn't have their own fleets of trains or trucks to move products all over the country.

Nestlé expanded in the twentieth century to become one of Europe's biggest makers of chocolate.

In Europe, Cadbury and Nestlé became huge corporations that dominated the chocolate market. With each passing year, these two companies—founded by men who had helped create the chocolate business—continued to buy up smaller companies founded by men who had had similar goals and dreams. Cadbury focused on selling in the countries that were part of the British Empire, such as Australia, Canada, India, and Scotland. It had almost no competition in the English-speaking world outside of America. For Nestlé, the demand for its baby-food products all over the world, even in the United States, meant that its salespeople had an open door through which they could also sell chocolate.

Hershey was the biggest producer of chocolate candy in North America, with Mars right behind it. Mars was still Hershey's biggest business customer, followed by Reese's. But even Hershey was looking to expand. It started buying up smaller companies and eventually bought Reese's.

Mars, Inc.—the American company founded by Frank—was still under the control of Frank's second wife and her daughter. Ousted son Forrest believed he could run the company better than they were, and during the war years had sought to convince them that he should take over. They were having none of his arguments and kept Forrest away.

The death of Ethel V. Mars in 1945 ended up being Forrest's golden ticket. While she was alive, the entire Mars company had been owned by Ethel and her daughter. But oddly, Frank Mars had specified in his will that half of Ethel's ownership should go to Forrest when she died. Unlike Milton Hershey, who had no family and wanted to share his wealth with those less fortunate than him, Frank Mars wanted to make sure that his company and his wealth never left the Mars family . . . ever. Suddenly Forrest owned a big chunk of Mars, Inc.

Forrest Mars.

The people who ran Mars, including relatives of Ethel who were none too fond of Forrest, worked for the next five years to prevent him from having any say in the business. Lawyers and lawsuits were involved, and Forrest fought to gain some control over Mars.

Meanwhile, things were going slowly over at M&M's. The huge business that had developed during the war—with its lucrative contracts—had slowed down, and Forrest was furious. He blamed Bruce Murrie, and in a fit of anger fired Murrie from their partnership and removed him from the company. (Forrest owned 80 percent of the company, so he could get away with it.)

The move shocked nearly everyone. The Murrie family had been very generous to Forrest, and the Hershey Chocolate Company had always worked hand in hand with the Mars family. Forrest didn't care. What mattered to him was full control of the M&M's brand, and by 1949 he had it. He changed the name of the company to Food Manufacturers, Inc. and added his English-based Mars bar and pet food companies to it. Now he had all his personal companies in one place. But that didn't keep him from wanting his father's company, too.

The following year, tired of all the legal fighting, the Mars executives agreed to give in to Forrest's demands. They offered him a third of the company, enough that he could start making decisions about its future.

First, he expanded the factory to produce more Milky Ways, Snickers, and 3 Musketeers. Second, he brought in equipment that manufactured the candies much faster and more uniformly, using conveyor belts. Then he installed machines to wrap the thousands upon thousands of candy bars that Mars, Inc. was making every day; surprisingly, for a company as huge as Mars, candy had still been wrapped by hand.

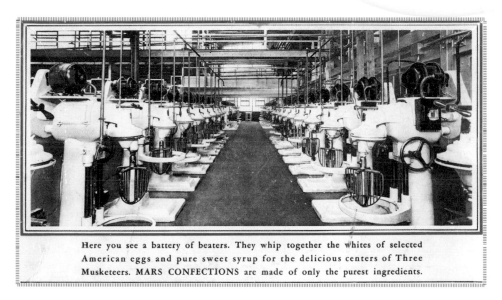

Here you see a battery of beaters. They whip together the whites of selected American eggs and pure sweet syrup for the delicious centers of Three Musketeers. MARS CONFECTIONS are made of only the purest ingredients.

Mars became the world's biggest chocolate manufacturer in part by modernizing the equipment in its factories.

When Forrest got through modernizing, he had accomplished an amazing feat: he had turned his father's company into the largest maker of chocolate candy bars in the world. But as big as Mars had become, it was one of the most mysterious corporations in America. Since it was family run, it didn't have to tell the public or stockholders how much money it made or who its customers were. It never allowed reporters inside its factories to do stories on how it ran its business. Forrest didn't even allow anyone to take pictures of him (he made an exception for his company photograph). Most people outside Mars, Inc. didn't know what he looked like, including some of his biggest customers. Forrest was obsessed with maintaining control of all aspects of his personal and professional life.

But he still didn't have complete control of Mars. For the next decade, he fought with his half sister and her family (her uncle, her husband, and others) to become the one person who ran the business. At the same time, Food Manufacturers Inc. had become almost as big as Mars, Inc. thanks to its pet food business and successful brands such as Uncle Ben's Rice. Plus, Forrest had finally gotten M&M's back on track.

Little known fact: The white Ms on M&M's are printed on each candy as they pass under soft printer rollers.

The candies had always been incredibly popular with kids but didn't have the same appeal with parents, who felt that buying—or giving—larger chocolate bars was a better value. Forrest had to convince adults that there was something truly special about M&M's.

It turns out that all it took was a single advertising slogan, one that captured the reason Forrest had become intrigued by the candy in the first place. He and his advertising agency came up with the phrase "Melts in your mouth, not in your hand." Suddenly all those parents who had messy chocolate and stained clothes and dark fingerprints to clean up during the summer—air-conditioning was still a rarity in America—realized they had a good reason to buy M&M's. They could give their kids chocolate and not have to clean up after them. With M&M's, everyone got what they wanted. Sales soared, and demand for the multicolored candy poured in from nearly every corner of the world.

Forrest kept pressing his half sister, and finally, in 1964, she sold him her share of Mars, Inc. She was sick from cancer and was tired of the years of fighting. One of her conditions to sell, though, was that Forrest always keep the company name as Mars, and not change it to Food Manufacturers Inc. He agreed.

Now that the company was all Forrest's, he did something he'd always wanted to do. He told executives at the Hershey Chocolate Company that he would no longer do any business with them. Instead, he would make his own chocolate . . . and from now on would view Hershey as a major competitor.

The last great partnership in the chocolate world came to an end. And that's where it stands today. The four biggest names in chocolate—Cadbury, Nestlé, Hershey, and Mars—control more than two-thirds of all the chocolate candy sold in the United States and half of what is sold in the rest of the world. They are all competing for your sweet tooth and your taste buds. Among them, they have hundreds of familiar chocolate brand names that you see every time you walk into a supermarket, convenience store, drugstore, gas station, or deli.

There are many smaller brands still alive, with new ones starting up every year. These newcomers are usually sold in specialty stores, and sometimes only regionally—just as chocolate was sold decades ago. We'll talk about the new crop of chocolate makers, and how they are turning away from milk chocolate, in a later chapter.

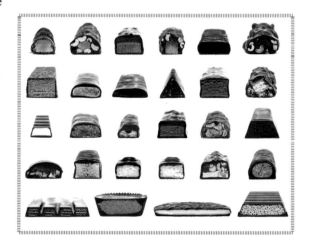

The sheer number of chocolate bars available today is mind-boggling, with hundreds of choices.

CHOCOLATE SPREADS OUT

AS MUCH AS WE THINK OF CHOCOLATE AS A TYPE of candy, there are dozens of other foods that have been changed dramatically by chocolate. In some cases, those foods wouldn't be the same without chocolate.

Take brownies. Today it's almost impossible to think of a brownie as anything but chewy and chocolate. In the late 1800s, though, they were more like a cake and contained no chocolate at all. They used molasses as their main flavoring—which is what made them brown.

In 1896 a woman in Massachusetts named Fannie Farmer wrote a unique cookbook called *The Boston Cooking-School Cook Book*. It wasn't the first cookbook, but it *was* the first to outline how important it was to use exact measurements in recipes. Prior to Farmer's book, cooks were used to "cupfuls" and "spoonfuls"

The first brownies didn't have any chocolate. They were made with molasses.

of ingredients, regardless of the size of those cups or spoons. To many people in the kitchen, a spoonful one day could be a huge serving spoon, and the next day, for a different recipe, it might be a tiny teaspoon.

Farmer's book was so well received that it changed the way people approached baking from then on. In some ways, it was more important for its attention to the details of cooking than for the actual recipes. The cookbook sold out, and Fannie had a new version printed in 1906. Buried inside the new cookbook was one recipe that would become a chocolate staple around the world.

This was the age of powdered cocoa, before milk chocolate and candy bars had become a phenomenon. Most people still thought of chocolate as something you drank, although cooks everywhere had started adding cocoa to pastries and ice cream.

What Fannie Farmer did was create a recipe for brownies that substituted chocolate for some of the flour. She used unsweetened chocolate, so the sweetness of the brownie came from sugar, and not the chocolate itself. But reducing the amount of flour and adding chocolate created a thick, dark treat that was less like cake, and chewier than cookies. Ever since, brownies have been synonymous with chocolate.

A few years later, in 1912 to be exact, the world's most popular manufactured cookie was invented—and it contained chocolate. The National Biscuit Company—later known as Nabisco—had risen to national prominence with the success of its "blond" cookies, better known as Barnum's Animal Crackers.

Animal Crackers were popular cookies in America before chocolate was used in making cookies.

But chocolate was becoming a popular flavor in America, and Milton Hershey's new milk chocolate bars were changing the way Americans consumed it. Bakers at the National Biscuit Company decided to make a chocolate cookie.

Using the Dutch method—which creates very dark chocolate with not much sweetness—they made a nearly black wafer cookie embossed with a circular design of clovers and a ridged edge, like coins had. They sandwiched solid sweet cream in between two of the wafers, and created a cookie they called the Oreo.

No one is sure where the name Oreo came from; it could be from the French word for gold, which is *or*. It might be the Greek word for mountain, which is *oreo*. Or it might have been a clever four-letter word that sounded good. No one knows. However, it was a better name than Hydrox. That was the name given to a cookie invented right before the Oreo, which was so similar that it might have been the inspiration for the Oreo. But the name Hydrox—

Oreos are one of the most popular cookies ever invented. Dark Dutch chocolate gives the two wafers their distinctive taste.

a combination of the words *hydrogen* and *oxygen*, the ingredients in fresh air—sounded like something in a chemistry set.

The combination of chocolate cookie and cream center is important to our story because the Oreo wafer still tastes pretty much the way it did more than a hundred years ago. If you eat just the cookie part—not the cream—you'll get a sense of what the first chocolate confectioneries were like. It's not sweet like chocolate candy (the Oreo's sweetness comes from the sugary filling), and it even has a tiny trace of the bitterness that's part of the natural flavor of cocoa.

When it comes to sweet chocolate, especially in baking, we have to mention chocolate chips. Most of the kitchens in America have them, and they are used for making everything from fudge to cake to ice cream. Perhaps most important, they are the essential component for making chocolate chip cookies. In a backward twist of fate, it was the invention of the chocolate chip cookie that led to the invention of the chocolate chip.

As we've seen with many good chocolate stories, this one has a few different versions. The one thing that everyone agrees on is that Ruth Wakefield invented the chocolate chip cookie around 1930.

Ruth and her husband lived in Whitman, Massachusetts, where they ran an old-fashioned inn called the Toll House. Ruth, a trained dietician, did the cooking and was meticulous about her recipes, much like Fannie Farmer. She had her own specialty: the Butter Drop Do sugar cookie, which she made in big batches for her guests. Occasionally she would add baking chocolate—the dark, unsweetened version—to these cookies to give them a cocoa flavor.

The first story states that one day, as she was making the cookies, Ruth realized that she had run out of baking chocolate. All she had on hand was a bar of Nestlé's Semi-Sweet chocolate. Ruth took an ice pick to the bar, broke it up, and threw the "chocolate morsels" into the batter. After she took the cookies out of the oven, she found that some of the morsels had not fully melted. Not wanting to waste a batch—another recurring theme in the history of chocolate—she served them anyway. Her guests loved this accidental cookie, and clamored for more. She went back and repeated the process. The chocolate chip cookie was born.

Now for the other story, which begins the same way. Ruth was making a batch of her sugar cookies for the guests staying at the Toll House. Since she made such large batches, she had a huge automatic mixing bowl to stir the dough. On this particular occasion, the mixer was vibrating so much that an unwrapped bar of Nestlé's Semi-Sweet chocolate, which was stored on a shelf above the bowl, fell in. The mixer ground it up in an instant, spreading chocolate "morsels" throughout the batter. Ruth couldn't pick the pieces out of the dough, so decided to bake it anyway. When her guests tried it, they loved it.

Regardless of the real story, people heard about Ruth's new

Chocolate chips might have been created by a kitchen accident at the Toll House Inn.

cookies and began stopping at the Toll House to try them. A local Boston newspaper even printed the recipe. The thing that made this chocolate creation different from others was that anyone with a kitchen could make it. Since many households already baked their own cookies, it was a simple matter to go out and buy a Nestlé Semi-Sweet chocolate bar to make this incredible new cookie.

Sales of the Nestlé Semi-Sweet bar rose quickly after the publication of the recipe. The Nestlé company wanted to make sure that its competitors—like Hershey—didn't start trying to sell their own semi-sweet bars to people who wanted to make the cookies. So representatives of Nestlé approached Ruth Wakefield with a deal: they would provide her with all the chocolate she would ever need for free . . . in return for allowing Nestlé to print her actual recipe for Toll House Cookies on the wrapper of the Semi-Sweet bar. (One version of this story has "Andrew Nestlé himself" giving her the chocolate. The problem is that there never was an Andrew Nestlé, and the Nestlé company was in fact a huge corporation that had been sold away decades before by Henri Nestlé.)

Nestlé modified its bar for cookie makers by making little notches in the chocolate and providing a small cutting tool in the package to help break it into smaller pieces. Even this wasn't easy enough for home bakers, so the company came up with tiny, ready-to-use bits that it called chocolate morsels. The rest of the world called them chocolate chips.

To this day, every bag of Nestlé chocolate chips is labeled as containing "morsels" and features the original Toll House recipe. The chocolate chip cookie is the most popular cookie in America, and there are claims that more than seven billion of them are made every year in the United States alone.

While cooks were experiencing happy chocolate accidents in America, one man in Italy was taking an entirely different approach to what chocolate could do.

As we've seen, World War II affected the availability of cocoa all over the world. As war spread throughout Europe in the 1940s, a pastry maker in Italy named Pietro Ferrero could not get nearly enough chocolate for his bakery. In order to make his chocolate go a little further each day, he began mixing it with hazelnut paste. Hazelnut paste was like a sweet peanut butter, and when mixed with chocolate it had a unique flavor that wasn't quite chocolate and not quite hazelnut, but a tasty blend of both.

He sold his concoction in sandwich form, spreading it between slices of bread and selling it to local families for lunches. Ferrero soon learned that many children were eating only the inside of the sandwich and throwing the bread away. This convinced him to sell the spread by itself, and soon his customers were buying only the spread, not the sandwiches. Since the hazelnut-chocolate mixture was much cheaper than anything made of pure chocolate, it was easier for people in war-torn Italy to afford. After World War II, Ferrero's son sold the paste in jars and it became popular throughout Europe as Nutella—"nut" from hazelnut, and "ella," a pleasant-sounding Italian suffix.

The popularity of Nutella chocolate-and-hazelnut spread has made the Ferreros one of the richest families in Europe.

Today the Ferreros are Italy's version of the Mars family. They control one of the biggest candy empires in the world, they are the country's richest family, and they closely guard the original recipes created by Pietro. Nutella is one of the world's most popular spreads—the company makes enough jars every year to circle the equator one and a half times. Many Europeans, and more and more Americans, include Nutella in their daily breakfasts, using it in place of jam, jelly, syrup, or butter.

From bars and wafers to cookies and spreads, chocolate can now be found in thousands of different foods. Millions, perhaps billions, of products are produced every day. Let's find out how all this chocolate gets made.

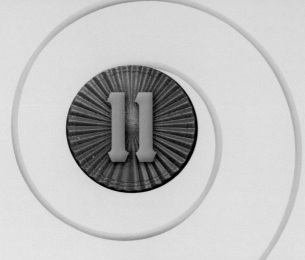

FROM BEAN TO BAR

THE GREAT PARADOX OF CHOCOLATE PRODUCTION is that it is a complicated blend of simple ingredients: cocoa butter, cocoa powder, sugar, and milk. The ingredients are about as basic as cooking gets; the production is about as complicated as any in the entire food world.

White chocolate drops being coated with a milk chocolate covering.

Chocolate is made everywhere from giant factories processing tons of beans per day to tiny shops that craft their chocolate by hand. Some factories produce more than a million bars a day just to keep up with demand, and are monstrously huge, resembling small cities. They have to be big not only because they must produce so many chocolates but because there are so many steps required to make good chocolate.

Chocolate factories are found all over the world. Hershey, for instance, has nine facilities in the United States alone. Specific factories produce specific candy, such as the Hershey plant in Stuarts Draft, Virginia, which makes Reese's Pieces and Almond Joy bars. Hershey also has factories in Canada, Mexico, India, Brazil, Malaysia, and China. Ferrero, which is a smaller company than Hershey, has eighteen factories of its own around the world. Nestlé and Cadbury each have dozens across the globe.

So let's take a walk through a typical milk chocolate factory.

The first thing you notice is the overwhelming smell of chocolate. Because chocolate making requires so much cocoa powder, it's inevitable that some of this powder drifts invisibly into the air. These tiny particles float around the factory, giving it a strong aroma that pervades and surrounds the building. In some chocolate-factory towns, you can smell the chocolate for miles.

Specialized machines are used in each stage of chocolate production.

Another thing you'll notice is that much of the machinery inside the factory is white, silver, or light colored. This is to allow workers to check on the machinery for chocolate spills or the accumulation of dirt, both of which are very bad for chocolate making. In order to keep the presence of dirt down, factories usually require workers to wear hairnets and robes while working inside.

It is also loud in the factory, because machines used for grinding beans or wrapping and packing candy bars have lots of mechanical parts that are constantly in motion. For most companies, these machines are one of a kind, specially designed and built just for their chocolates. The Hershey Company can't, for example, buy the machines that make Mars's M&M's, nor can Mars, Inc. buy the machines that make Hershey's Kisses. The design and operations of these machines are almost as important to each company as the recipes.

The factory receives daily shipments of the most important ingredients needed for making chocolate: cocoa beans, milk, and sugar.

Surprisingly, out of all these ingredients, the most critical one is milk. No matter where a chocolate factory is, it typically has to have cocoa products and sugar shipped in from other parts of the world, usually from Africa, southern Asia, or Central America. Cocoa and sugar travel well, and don't spoil quickly. That, however, is not true of milk. It has to be collected from dairy cows every day and processed right away to get rid of bacteria, and then quickly refrigerated to keep it fresh. Even then, and under the best of conditions, milk only lasts a few weeks. Because chocolate factories require an enormous amount of fresh milk every day—tens of thousands of gallons—they need a nearby supply.

Dairy milk comes from dairy cows, and dairy cows thrive in moderate climates that also support lots of fresh grass and grains. Nearly every European and North American country has dairy cows; they are especially prevalent

Access to dairy cows is very important in making milk chocolate.

in the American Midwest, England, Switzerland, and Germany. This is why the biggest advances in milk chocolate and chocolate production occurred in these areas—there was access to all the milk that the chocolate makers needed.

Other regions of the world, in places as vastly different from one another as Scandinavia and Australia, also have dairy cows. They don't have as many as America or Western Europe, in part because their climates make many areas of the country inhospitable to dairy cows. Despite the smaller numbers of cows, these regions still have their own milk chocolate cultures, with confections featuring local spices and flavors.

Interestingly, two places that have almost no history of milk chocolate creation are Asia and Africa. At first glance, you might guess that this has to do with their access to modern technology or their level of business interaction with the rest of the world. The truth is that the vast majority of the

The countries that have the most milk production are also the countries that produce the most milk chocolate.

land in those two continents has no dairy cows. Most of their cattle are used as beasts of burden or for meat. Historically, their milk comes from animals like goats and yaks, neither of which produce milk suitable for chocolate. Making it stranger still, Africa is the largest producer of cocoa beans—yet its people eat almost no chocolate of any kind.

That hasn't stopped people in countries like Japan and Egypt from wanting modern milk chocolate, though, and that chocolate has to come from somewhere. Multinational companies with huge factories that can ship chocolate all over the world are the answer.

Back to our factory and its milk supply. A large chocolate manufacturing plant will take delivery of more than 250,000 gallons of milk a day. A typical dairy cow produces about eight gallons of milk every day, which means that this one factory is bringing in the milk from thirty thousand cows—every single day.

Large metal tanker trucks transport milk from farms to chocolate factories.

Once it arrives at the factory in special tanker trucks, the milk is mixed with sugar. Like cocoa beans, sugar is used by the truckload and train-load for making chocolate, and it is also used for innards like nougat and marshmallow. Every twenty-four hours, the U.S. chocolate industry goes through eight million pounds of sugar.

During the blending of the milk and sugar, much of the milk's water is evaporated—using heat and pressure—to eliminate it. Getting rid of the water early in the process is essential to making sure that the rest of the manufacturing goes smoothly. As the water disappears, the milk and sugar are continually stirred together until they form a substance like taffy or soft caramel.

In a different part of the factory, the cocoa beans are being processed. Cocoa beans arrive less frequently than milk because they can be stored longer and don't need to be handled as often. Several thousand tons of beans are delivered to the factory each month—usually by train—which means millions of pounds of beans are stored there at any given time. This is because it takes about four hundred beans to create just one pound of chocolate.

As we know, cocoa beans come from inside the huge pods of the cocoa tree. There are actually three different kinds of cocoa trees: the Forastero, the Criollo, and the Trinitario. Close to 85 percent of the world's chocolate comes from Forastero cocoa trees, while only 3 percent comes from the rare Criollo cocoa bean. The third tree, a hybrid of these two called the Trinitario, provides just over 10 percent of the world's cocoa. Forastero trees tend to be the hardiest and produce the most beans, so they make up most of the world's planta-tions. Criollo trees are much more fragile, and produce a less bitter bean, so its beans are used for the most expensive chocolates.

Regardless of the type of tree, the pods are picked as soon as they ripen. The average tree produces about fifty pods a year, which comes out to about 2,500 beans. Once the pods are harvested, they are split open, and the beans are pulled out along with their pulp. The beans are fermented, dried, and then packed up in sacks for shipping.

The plantation owner sells the cocoa crop for about fifty cents a pound to "middlemen," businesses that buy beans from many different plantations and then warehouse them all in large buildings. From these warehouses, the beans are exported or sold directly to large chocolate compa-nies. They are loaded on container ships and trans-ported to Europe, Asia, Australia, and America. When they reach their desti-nation ports, they are then shipped by rail or by truck to the factories, where they are stored in silos and huge bins.

MAIN EXPORTERS IN MILLIONS OF TONS

Cote d'Ivoire 1.51 m
Ghana 1.02m
Indonesia .45m
Nigeria .24m
Cameroon .23m
Brazil, Ecuador, Togo, Dominican Republic, Papua New Guinea < .2m

EXPORT DESTINATIONS IN MILLIONS OF TONS

Netherlands .72m
U.S. .45m
Germany .32m
Malaysia .27m
Belgium .17m
France, U.K., Spain, Singapore, Italy < .14m

Cocoa beans are grown in the areas marked in orange, but shipped for chocolate production primarily to the regions marked in red.

By the time those beans are sold as chocolate in stores, the fifty cents paid to the plantation owner for a single pound will have gone up to more than ten dollars a pound. The cost goes up because every business that comes into con-tact with the beans needs to make a profit. The middlemen, the exporters, the

Workers unloading bags of cocoa beans from the hold of a ship.

Warehouses store the beans before they are delivered to chocolate factories.

factories, the distributors, and the retailers all raise the price of what they are selling in order to get their share.

Once the beans get to the factory, they are handled almost exclusively by machines and computers. Except for small specialty chocolate makers, the days of grinding and mixing chocolate ingredients by hand are long gone. Machines control the process, with humans making sure that nothing goes wrong. Everything is electronically measured, checked for quality, and weighed so at the end each individual product comes out looking like every other individual product.

Back to the factory where the chocolate is being made.

When the cocoa beans are ready to be used, they are transferred from the storage silos and bins to conveyor belts. These moving belts first take the beans through a quick cleaning. This is done with puffs of air, magnets (to pull up any pieces of metal that might have entered the bags), and screens (to sift out small particles like pebbles and dirt).

The belt continues to the roasters. These are large rotating ovens that roast the beans at temperatures from 130 degrees Fahrenheit on up to 500 degrees. Depending on the size of the batch, roasting can last from a few minutes to more

A cocoa bean roaster.

than an hour. Like all things chocolate, whether it is the design of the machines or the prized recipes, the exact temperatures and the exact amount of time for roasting are secrets protected by each company.

The beans are roasted in order to give them more flavor—the same thing is done with coffee beans—and also to dry them out. After they are dried and cooled, the bean shells are brittle and are easily broken. The beans are then moved along to a breaking chamber. Here they are passed between rollers that crack the shells. Once that happens the beans are flung against the chamber's steel walls, and the shells separate from the inner nib. In a process called winnowing, a complex series of screens, sieves, jets of air, and vacuuming devices makes sure that the shells get completely removed from the conveyor belt, allowing just the nibs to continue on.

The nibs, which are again cleaned and checked for any foreign particles like stubborn shells, are then ground up under heavy moving weights called grinders. The force of these weights crushes the nibs into the paste known as cocoa mass (or chocolate liquor, depending on who is running the factory).

CHOCOLATE MANUFACTURING PROCESS

•1•
INGREDIENTS OF CHOCOLATE

COCOA MASS

COCOA BUTTER

SUGAR

MILK POWDER

•2•
MIXING
The ingredients are mixed to form a chocolate paste.

•3•
REFINING
Breaks down the tiny particles of milk, cocoa, and sugar into the finest powder with giant rollers.

•4•
CONCHING
Removes moisture and develops specific flavor of chocolate.

Top: Cocoa butter after it has been removed from the cocoa mass.

Bottom: Cocoa cake "pucks" have almost no cocoa butter and are ready to be mixed with milk and sugar.

The mass itself is poured into molds in a machine called a cocoa butter press. It is then pressed even harder to squeeze the cocoa butter out of the mass. Most of the liquid cocoa butter, which looks like corn oil, is drained off, leaving a dark, solid piece of cocoa powder with only a small amount of cocoa butter. This bit of cocoa cake resembles an oversize hockey puck.

These "pucks" are then broken up and added to the sugar/milk mixture that was created in another part of the building. Together, they are cooked in vats until they become a thick brown syrup. After the syrup is completely mixed, it is dried out in ovens. This results in a grainy powder, somewhat similar in texture to sand, called chocolate crumb.

The crumb then passes through yet another set of crushing steel rollers to make sure that each little particle is the right size. If the particles are too large, the chocolate will taste gritty, like it has sand in it. If the particles are too small, the chocolate will feel oily. The crumb grinder is designed to create something called "a unique chocolate particle size" that will create the perfect chocolate texture. It ends up feeling very similar to baby powder.

The crumb continues through the factory along the conveyor belt until it comes to large vats. At this point, it is mixed back into some of the cocoa butter that was pressed out earlier—a process that goes back to the method the Fry brothers developed back in the 1840s. The crumb and the cocoa butter are blended and then churned for a long time in a conching machine, modeled on the one Rodolphe Lindt invented. It has large mixing blades that stir the combined ingredients to ensure that they are completely smooth without any lumps.

At this stage, temperature and time are extremely important. The right combination will determine how hard and how glossy the final chocolate is. The bar should be hard enough to snap, but not so hard that it is difficult to break. And the surface should be glossy with a bit of shine, but not greasy.

Conching can last anywhere from an hour to nearly an entire day, depending on the recipe. After the conching, the mixture passes through one more sieve to filter out any lumps that might have escaped.

Now, finally, we have chocolate. To be precise, we have warm, liquid, velvety *milk* chocolate. Yet, despite everything that it's taken to get here, we still have to pour it, shape it, and give it an identity.

The warm chocolate is flowed into large containers fitted with external injector tubes. These containers are high up off the floor, often about ceiling height. Underneath them runs a nonstop highway of molds, all the same shape and size. As they flow under the chocolate containers, the molds stop long enough to have a burst of chocolate

Above: A conch stirs the chocolate mixture for many hours.

Right: Warm liquid chocolate flows into containers before being molded.

squirted into them by the injector tubes. Think of it as being like cars stopping briefly at a tollbooth on a highway before moving on again. The moment the molds are filled with chocolate—and it takes barely a second—they move quickly on down the line.

As they go, the molds are vibrated on the conveyor belt to make sure the chocolate levels off. Vibrating also releases any air bubbles that might have

Top: The containers are kept filled with chocolate while molds pass underneath.

Bottom: Injectors underneath the containers place exact amounts of chocolate into molds.

been injected into the mold. This happens before the chocolate cools down and gets too hard. (By the way, if the chocolate has a logo or a name stamped on it, that comes from raised lettering on the bottom of the mold, which presses up into the chocolate, making the inset lettering or logo you see when you unwrap it. The top of the mold on the belt is actually the bottom of the chocolate bar.)

For the next half hour or so, the chocolate moves slowly along the conveyor belt. It cools down and hardens, going from a liquid state to a solid state. If the chocolate cools down too slowly, it will be mushy when it comes out of the molds. If it cools down too quickly, the cocoa butter separates and turns parts of the bar a white powdery color. This is called chocolate bloom. While it doesn't hurt the bar, bloom isn't attractive and takes away from the sheen of the chocolate. Sometimes you'll see bloom on bars that have absorbed moisture because they've been too long on the shelf.

As the bar cools, the cocoa butter is solidifying, and its fat molecules take on a crystalline structure. Controlling the temperature to the precise degree during this process is called tempering. If the temperature isn't at the correct level, it causes poorly formed crystals, which can make the chocolate soft or crumbly. The right temperature creates a solid that holds together firmly but not so firmly that it's unbreakable.

While it is cooling, the chocolate continues to move along the conveyor belts. Once it has cooled, the chocolate hits the end of this production line. It is flipped out of the molds, sort of like people getting off at the end of an escalator. This

Left: Molds travel along a conveyor belt as the chocolate cools.

Below: Once the chocolate is cool, the molds are flipped over to release the candy.

turns the bars right side up, and they drop to another conveyor belt that lines them up one after another and makes sure they are the right weight and color. This belt leads to the wrapping machines.

For most of chocolate candy's early history, it was wrapped by hand in paper or foil. In the 1950s, machines were invented that automated this process, usually wrapping the chocolates first in thin aluminum foil, and then again with a paper wrapper that had the bar's information and the company's logo printed on it. (The Hershey's bar and Cadbury Dairy Milk bar are examples of this.) The foil was used to ensure freshness, but it couldn't be printed on—the ink would rub off—so the paper wrapper was used to identify the bar. In the last decade or so, technology has advanced so that it is now possible to print all the information right on the foil itself. This eliminates the need for the paper band over the aluminum. Most manufacturers have switched to wrapping the chocolate just in printed foil or a thin plastic wrap.

The foil is preprinted with the bar's name, the company logo, and the list of ingredients. It arrives in the factory on huge rolls. The foil is then spooled out at incredibly high speeds underneath the conveyor belt. It's like a roll of paper towels being unraveled as quickly as possible. The foil moves through openings in the conveyor belt and is cut into shape just as the chocolate goes over it. The wrapper is pushed up and around the chocolate and then sealed. This is all done

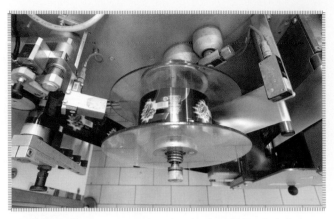

Special machines wrap each individual candy with foil at incredibly high speed.

by astoundingly complex machines with fast-moving arms and cutters. Some of these machines can wrap several hundred candies a minute—three or four a second. At that speed, you can barely see it happen.

The wrapped chocolate continues to its final destination. A narrow conveyor sends it down an aisle where robot "hands" with suckers on the end of each "finger" pick up the bars one by one and rapidly lift them from the belt. They are raised and swung away from the line into waiting boxes. As the boxes are filled, they are sent to another conveyor belt to be packed into large cartons. They head out to the factory loading dock and are loaded into train cars or trucks. Then they travel for hundreds, sometimes thousands, of miles until they are delivered to your local store.

That's a lot of work just to get chocolate from the tropical jungles to your mouth, isn't it? And we're describing only solid milk chocolate. We haven't even taken into account some of the more intricate chocolate bars you might have a taste for. For example, what about things like Kit Kats and Butterfingers and Milky Ways? How are those chocolate bars, with their unusual insides, even made?

Those bars actually start out as something else before the chocolate is ever

The wrapped candies are then sent to be packaged in boxes. Can you see the one candy that was missed by the wrapping machine? This almost never happens.

added—the insides are a candy in their own right. Kit Kats start as thin sugar wafers, Butterfingers are a shard-like mixture of peanut butter and caramel, and Milky Ways are a not-quite-solid nougat. Each of these "insides" is made and assembled using its own recipe and complicated equipment. Once they've come off their conveyor belts and out of their own molds, they are sent on a different conveyor belt through a waterfall of chocolate. The warm chocolate flows in a sheet down over the belt, coating every piece that runs underneath it. The candy then runs over the top of a river of chocolate to make sure it is coated on the bottom. It's not quite Willy Wonka's river of chocolate, though; the chocolate flows in a controlled area in precise amounts to coat the candy perfectly and not let any go to waste.

In some ways, coating candy with chocolate is even harder than producing a solid bar. Consider Kit Kats, Twix, Violet Crumble, 5th Avenue, or any type of bar that is advertised as being crispy and crunchy. They have wafers or a very dry nougat inside. In order to stay crisp, they can't get wet or soggy. Yet, molten chocolate is very wet, and these candies are covered with it. In order not to ruin the insides, the warm liquid chocolate has to go on quickly and has to be cooled and dried almost immediately so as not to soak into the candy innards. This requires split-second timing among the machinery that pours, cools, dries, and moves the bar. And it works, millions of times a day.

There are more than a hundred billion M&M's made each year. That's a huge number, but there are a lot of huge numbers in the chocolate business. Another huge number: every minute, sixty thousand Hershey's Kisses are made. When you start adding it all up, thousands of tons of chocolate candy are being manufactured every single day. Just as impressive is that most of that chocolate is consumed within just a few days or weeks of it being produced. Some of us are eating more than a dozen pounds of chocolate a year—and the United States has one of the lower rates of chocolate consumption.

Why do we eat so much chocolate? Well, it's delicious, but there's more to our chocolate craving than taste. Part of our desire comes from what chocolate does to our brains.

12

COCOA CHEMISTRY

CHOCOLATE, IN ALL ITS MANY FORMS, IS THE most popular type of confection in the world. By all accounts, chocolate is also the most frequently craved food in the world. And while many of us think of chocolate as simply a great-tasting treat, the reality is that chocolate is one of the most complex chemical combinations known to man. As of the most recent research, there are more than six hundred known chemical compounds in raw chocolate, ranging from theobromine to caffeine. In fact, there may be more than a thousand chemical compounds; scientists are constantly finding more.

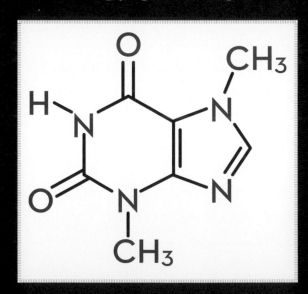

Theobromine, the naturally occurring chemical found in cocoa, is represented by the formula $C_7H_8N_4O_2$.

The reason that we don't know the exact number is that the chemistry of chocolate changes at every single stage of its production. Cocoa beans change their composition as they ferment—before they leave the plantation; nibs change from the heat during roasting; cocoa butter changes when it's separated from the mass. Of course, it all changes again many times over the moment other ingredients and their own unique chemistries are added to the final mix: sugar, milk, spices, fruits, or whatever is making up the final product. Cocoa beans are so complex in nature that scientists haven't been able to come up with a substitute for them (as they have for sugar). The carob pod, which grows on treelike bushes in hot climates, has a slightly chocolate taste and is used by some people as an alternative to chocolate in baking. But even carob can't produce a fraction of the taste sensations that chocolate does.

Figuring out what makes chocolate so appealing to humans is like constructing your own chemistry experiment. Even a very short list of what chocolate contains reads like a chemistry textbook.

THEOBROMINE · PHENYLETHYLAMINE · ANANDAMIDE
CAFFEINE · TRYPTOPHAN · **EPICATECHIN** · **DOPAMINE**
THIAMINE · RIBOFLAVIN · **MANGANESE** · CALCIUM
STEARIC ACID · **PALMITIC ACID** · OLEIC ACID · LINOLEIC ACID
IRON · **ZINC** · POTASSIUM · **COPPER XANTHINES**

Chief among these is theobromine. It is the primary chemical that comes from the cocoa seed and is named for the plant itself—remember, *theobroma* means "food of the gods." Theobromine is an alkaloid, a complex chemical substance created by plants, usually found in their seeds. Alkaloids have the unusual property of affecting the brain and central nervous system of mammals like humans and dogs. As such, they are often used to create medicines, but they can also be poisonous.

Given their effects on the brain, and depending on the plant, alkaloids can be used as stimulants or as sedatives. Notable alkaloids include morphine, which comes from the seeds of poppy plants; nicotine, which comes from the leaves of the tobacco plant; ephedrine, which comes from the ephedra plant; and caffeine, which comes from a number of sources, including coffee beans. Interestingly, regardless of their source or property, alkaloids tend to have a naturally bitter taste.

Theobromine has a mild stimulant effect on the brain, causing you to feel awake and alert. It also activates those parts of the brain that trigger feelings of pleasure. In addition, theobromine can stimulate the heart and increase your heart rate. It has been shown to help widen blood vessels, allowing for better blood flow and thus reducing blood pressure. Theobromine usually passes out of your system after six hours.

Speaking of pleasure, the brains of people in love have been shown to produce significant quantities of a chemical called phenylethylamine. It occurs naturally in the brain and is involved in the creation of feelings of pleasure and euphoria. Perhaps not surprisingly, phenylethylamine is also found in cocoa. The fact that eating chocolate means ingesting tiny amounts of phenylethlyamine might explain the relationship between chocolates and love, and why we give chocolates to people we love on special occasions—as opposed to giving them hamburgers or pizza. Chocolate might actually trigger the feeling of love.

Anandamide is another chemical found in cocoa that affects the brain. It is naturally produced by the brain and triggers reactions that

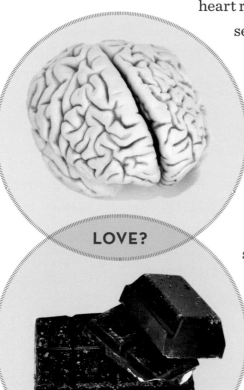

LOVE?

The pleasure we get from eating chocolate and the feeling of being in love are experienced in the same part of the brain.

cause the brain to suppress pain. Anandamide may improve a person's mood and feeling of well-being, possibly helping to alleviate depression. Interestingly, when the brain produces its own anandamide, it exists for only a short time before breaking down. When chocolate's anandamide enters the body, though, it tends to last longer than the brain's own. This might explain why chocolate makes us feel good while we're eating it. However, there is much more to learn about anandamide; the chemical was only discovered in 1992, and research is still ongoing.

There is also a tiny amount of caffeine in cocoa. It, too, has a stimulating effect on the central nervous system, and can cause wakefulness. However, there is so little theobromine and caffeine in the average bar of chocolate that it barely has any effect on humans.

The same is not true of theobromine and smaller mammals. Dogs, in particular, can be harmed by theobromine because their bodies don't break it down to a harmless chemical. Thus, the "food of the gods" is not the "food of the dogs." Always keep dogs separate from chocolate—they are not likely to enjoy the encounter.

These chemicals are in cocoa even before it's processed or turned into candy. The fact that many of them are stimulants probably accounts for why the earliest cocoa drinks were thought to be healthy for people and a cure for fatigue. Drinking it provided a mild jolt—like from coffee or a caffeinated soda—that might have given drinkers a quick burst of energy. Many scientists today think that people in ancient times ate cocoa beans because it made them feel good. Otherwise, there is very little explanation for why primitive tribes would have continued chewing on such a bitter seed and exploring other ways to ingest it. Such a theory—and it is only a theory, because no one knows for sure—explains why cocoa was savored and sought after for thousands of years before it ever became something sweet to eat.

While cocoa might be good for your brain, there are hundreds of other chemicals in cocoa that have positive effects on your body. For instance, cocoa is rich in a class of chemical called flavonoids. Although this sounds like it has something to do with flavor, it doesn't. Flavonoids (also referred to as flavonols) are believed to help blood vessels stay open and flexible, allowing for better blood flow. The better the blood flow, the easier it is for blood to circulate in the brain. Flavonols may help reduce damage to the brain from vessel-related injuries such as strokes.

Then there are polyphenols, a type of chemical that has antioxidant properties. Antioxidants are chemicals that fight free radicals, a type of molecule that causes the breakdown of cells as you age. Free radicals are known to have some links to Alzheimer's, cancer, and heart disease. The more antioxidants you have in your system, the better equipped your body is to protect its cells against these

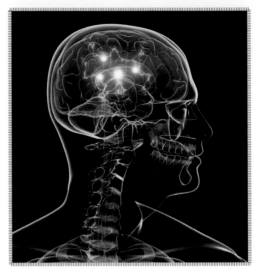

The ingredients in chocolate stimulate chemical reactions throughout our brains.

diseases. By the way, cocoa is not the only source of antioxidants—blackberries, raspberries, blueberries, cranberries, and pomegranates are all rich in them.

That's some of the good news about the health benefits of chocolate. Unfortunately, the news isn't entirely pleasant. The best health benefits from cocoa come right from the cocoa bean, before it's processed. For example, fermenting and roasting the beans removes significant amounts of the polyphenols.

Processing the bean, and adding sugar to it, diminish the levels of good chemical compounds. Which brings us to cocoa butter, a major component of milk chocolate. Cocoa butter is basically fat. As we know, fat isn't the best thing to be ingesting large quantities of. The same is true of the sugar used to make milk chocolate. The more cocoa butter and sugar that are mixed in with cocoa, the fewer health benefits it has—and the less "healthy" the chocolate becomes. The sweeter and richer the chocolate, the more it relies on those ingredients that are added to cocoa.

Scientific research over the past couple of decades has shown that there are health benefits to be derived from "natural" cocoa which has not been sweetened or subjected to so much processing. This has resulted in a growing interest in dark chocolate—chocolate that contains less milk and sugar and more cocoa powder or cocoa mass.

For years, dark chocolate was the ignored member of the chocolate bar family. Several companies, notably Hershey, have offered dark versions of their chocolate products for a long time. These were called semi-sweets, bittersweets, and dark chocolates. They had intense flavors, but they never came close to selling as much as the sweeter, richer candy. Many people, especially kids, thought these chocolates were bitter and had a slightly burned taste. They certainly didn't show up in too many Halloween bags or Easter baskets—and if they did, they were the very last things to be eaten.

Dark chocolate has much less milk and sugar, and a higher cocoa content, than other types of edible chocolate.

Dark chocolate saw its popularity suddenly soar as adults in the 1990s and early 2000s looked for types of chocolate that were more suitable to their tastes. Baby boomer adults (born between 1944 and 1964) were the first generation of consumers to grow up having milk chocolate their entire lives. But as people age, their tastes (and taste buds) change, and very sweet foods have less appeal. Boomers haven't wanted to give up chocolate, though. Especially not when the dark variety was being touted as a health food. So they've turned to dark chocolate as an alternative to the milk chocolate they grew up with.

Small boutique companies, similar to those tiny kitchen makers who existed a hundred years before, started making dark-chocolate bars. Essentially, dark chocolate leaves out the milk and much of the sugar from the candy bar. Dark chocolate is defined as having at least 35 percent of its content cocoa mass. That means a third of the chocolate has to come straight from the bean. There are some makers selling dark chocolate that is 80 to 90 percent cocoa mass content. Needless to say, at that level, chocolate can be incredibly bitter—almost as bitter as unsweetened baking chocolate.

The percentage of cocoa might not seem like a big deal to those of us who just like to eat chocolate. But manufacturers around the world must adhere to certain standards in order to call their products "chocolate," no matter what type of chocolate it is. For example, a typical milk chocolate bar has to have only 10 percent cocoa mass. The remaining 90 percent can be sugar, milk, and even vegetable oil. And "chocolate-flavored" or "chocolatey" foods are only related to chocolate because they use cocoa powder as a flavoring. They have no actual cocoa butter, and thus no chocolate, in them.

White chocolate, which is popular in its own right, isn't even chocolate. It is white because it has no cocoa powder in it—just raw cocoa butter with sugar and milk. The fact that it has some cocoa butter is the reason it is referred to as a form of chocolate. To make the whole concept even weirder, some manufacturers make white chocolate without using *any* cocoa butter at all—they simply use vegetable oil instead, which is much cheaper.

The three most popular forms of edible chocolate: dark, milk, and white. The only part of the cocoa bean contained in white chocolate is cocoa butter.

The use of vegetable oil in place of cocoa butter in regular chocolate has caused friction among countries selling and importing chocolate, especially in Europe. European countries wanted to define how much cocoa mass had to be in each bar in order for it to be called "real chocolate." They wanted anything that used vegetable oil to be called "chocolate substitute" or "chocolate flavored." Cadbury's Dairy Milk bar, for example, uses vegetable oil in its recipe—and more than a quarter of that bar's content is milk. It is considered the definitive British chocolate candy. But Switzerland, Belgium, and other countries don't think that vegetable oil, or so much milk, belongs in chocolate. They have fought for years to force Cadbury to call their bars something other than chocolate.

Chocolate contains any number of ingredients, with the most important being cocoa, milk, and sugar. The addition of various types of nuts and spices gives each chocolate bar its own unique flavor.

This has even extended to the United States. Mars uses the tagline "real chocolate" in its advertising, a not-so-subtle jab at Hershey, which uses sunflower oil and palm oil in some of its products, like Mr. Goodbar and Krackel. A lot of the cheaper "no name brand" chocolates you find during holidays have even less cocoa and cocoa butter in them, using large quantities of corn syrup and vegetable oil to keep the cost very low.

The fight over the definition of chocolate in Europe erupted into what became known as the "Chocolate Wars." These began in 1973 and lasted for three decades. Many countries limited the import, or entirely prevented the sale, of chocolate from rivals they felt were making inferior products. U.K. companies like Mars and Cadbury were actually banned from selling their chocolate in France, Belgium, Germany, the Netherlands, Greece, Italy, Luxembourg, and

Spain for twenty-seven years. No Mars bars, no Creme Eggs, no Kit Kats—they were illegal.

In 2000, most of these countries came to an agreement. The European Court of Justice determined that all chocolates must have a certain minimum of cocoa and cocoa butter content, and must be labeled accordingly. But the court also stated that adding vegetable oil does not make a chocolate bar any less of a chocolate bar—especially if people can read the ingredients on the label. By 2003 every European country was finally selling every other country's version of chocolate—whether they liked it or not.

In America, the Food and Drug Administration (FDA) has set guidelines since 1993 for how much cocoa mass has to be in each type of chocolate in order for it to be legally called chocolate. These are the amounts:

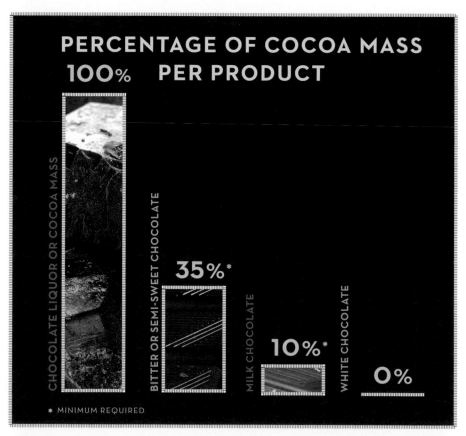

This chart shows how much cocoa mass (cocoa with the butter squeezed out) must be contained in different types of chocolate.

What this means is that you can see for yourself what is in the package (cocoa amounts are usually printed on the label—except for milk and white chocolate) and decide if you want to buy it and eat it. And that opens up a world of possibilities in which you can try chocolates of all types, flavors, and origins.

After all, it's only you who can decide what you like in a chocolate. And you have a lot to choose from. Chocolate has more than 1,500 flavor components, or "notes," that can be identified by professional tasters. Flavor notes are the qualities that make, say, barbecued ribs taste "smoky," "zesty," and "tangy," or that make lemonade "tart," "sour," and even "sweet," all in the same sip. Chocolate's notes range from spicy and floral to woody and bready.

Chocolate has so many notes in part because of the hundreds of different chemical compounds in it. Many of its flavors are accented by how long the original beans were roasted or fermented. Just as with coffee beans or a good melted cheese sandwich, heating draws out the flavor of beans. And just as heat is important to the beginning of chocolate's road to your mouth, heat is singularly important once that chocolate gets to your mouth. Why? Because it has to actually melt inside your mouth.

One of the reasons that chocolate tastes so good—and another reason for so many flavor notes—is its melting point. It is a solid when you pick it up, but once you put it in your mouth, it instantly begins melting. This is because your mouth is slightly warmer than chocolate's melting point.

The chocolate doesn't turn into a liquid right away, though. It gradually gets softer and less solid, which causes it to spread out slowly over your tongue and taste buds while still maintaining a thick and smooth texture. This is an enjoyable sensation, and it is called mouthfeel. A more scientific term for mouthfeel is "viscosity," the measure of thickness and flow. Chocolate—especially milk chocolate—melts nicely in your mouth because it contains very little water. The smooth liquid sensation comes from the cocoa butter actually starting to liquefy.

The term "mouthfeel" is something that food experts use to describe how we react to the texture of things we eat. Food experts, and chocolate fans, even have a process by which they recommend enjoying chocolate. It involves all five senses, and isn't something you can do with, say, burritos or gum.

Here is the recommended way to appreciate a solid chocolate bar. Try these steps in order . . . if you have the time and can resist popping it right into your mouth.

SOUND: First, break off a piece from the bar. Listen to what that sounds like. A good, fresh dark chocolate will "snap," while a good milk chocolate will have a quieter break, but not one that is mushy or completely silent.

FEEL: As you're holding the chocolate, notice the feel of it. It should not be greasy, slippery, or soft, or so hard that it feels like a piece of wood. Your fingers shouldn't sink into it, but they should be able to push in slightly with some pressure.

LOOK: Take a close look at the chocolate. It should be a deep—or rich—color. Milk chocolate is rich brown to slightly dark brown, while dark chocolate is just that—dark to almost black. Milk chocolate should have a nice finish that's almost-but-not-quite shiny. Some dark chocolates will have a sheen that's almost glossy but not slippery. Any chocolate with a white-brown-gray splotch is suffering from bloom. It's not bad and won't affect the taste, but it does mean the chocolate is either old or perhaps was not properly mixed or tempered during the manufacturing.

SMELL: Hold it up to your nose and breathe it in. Take a deep whiff. The aroma of every chocolate is different, so you'll be able to take in many flavor notes at once, ranging from hints of fruits or tree leaves to smoke and sugar. It also shouldn't be too sweet or overwhelming—like perfume—but should drift lightly in the air.

TASTE: Take a small bite of the chocolate. Don't chew it, but let it melt in your mouth. Notice how easily it dissolves without chewing. There should be no gritty sensation, and it should feel smooth and even silky against your tongue.

Take another bite, and this time chew it up gently, then let it melt in your mouth. You'll taste different things this time, such as sugar and vanilla and other ingredients, especially as the chocolate melts in different parts of your mouth. The presence of these other ingredients depends on the bar. Specialty bars include everything from chili powder and curry to bacon and salt, and each of these is more evident to your taste buds as you lightly chew it up.

Now you know how the professionals recommend checking out your chocolate. This process does help you to experience chocolate via your entire sensory system, letting your brain—and your body chemistry—take full advantage of everything the cocoa bean has to offer.

That said, nothing compares to putting a small piece of chocolate in your mouth, closing your eyes, and letting your taste buds do all the work.

Eating chocolate should be a delight to every one of your senses.

13

THE MODERN MAKERS

THE INTERNATIONAL COCOA ORGANIZATION in London lists more than nine hundred medium to large makers of chocolate around the world. This list includes the global giants like Nestlé, Hershey, Mars, Ferrero, and Cadbury, as well as smaller national companies with international followings, like Maison du Chocolat in Paris, Madre in Hawaii, and Vosges in Chicago. It also contains some well-known individual chocolatiers, like Jacques Torres in New York, who is known as Mr. Chocolate for his innovative creations, his TV show, and his cookbooks.

Many small chocolate shops specialize in small handmade candies like truffles.

Chocolatiers are a type of chocolate maker who create something unique out of chocolate using their own recipes. Most of them do not actually grind their own cocoa from beans. Rather, they purchase prepared chocolate from large companies and then melt it down and add their own touches to it.

(Mr. Torres is an exception; he does grind his own cocoa beans.) It might seem strange to think that chocolatiers buy their chocolate from someplace else, but it is quite common . . . and necessary. It's exactly like your local bakers. They don't own their own wheat fields or flour mills or granaries, and they don't own farms with eggs and milk. They buy wheat and yeast and dairy products in large quantities (from direct suppliers, not from the grocery store) in order to bake their own particular type of breads, cakes, cookies, croissants, and other goods.

A chocolatier pours liquid onto a slab to allow it to cool before shaping it.

The same is the case with chocolatiers. They buy chocolate from one of the many large companies that process cocoa beans. These companies are called cocoa grinders, and they are generally very large—and very unknown—food companies. The chocolatier can select from hundreds of different types of chocolate products from the cocoa grinders, using catalogs to pick and choose everything from the amount of cocoa in each ounce to the amount of sugar or the mixture of different types of beans. This chocolate is delivered to the chocolatier in the form of bars, disks, or pellets. Although there are dozens of these cocoa grinders, most of the chocolate that is sold to bakers, small chocolatiers, dessert makers, and restaurants comes from just three companies: Barry Callebaut, Cargill, and Olam.

There are a host of smaller grinders, many of whom cater to specific segments of the chocolate business. High-end grinders, for example, handle only certain kind of beans and are in demand by chocolatiers and restaurant chefs. Among these are France's Valrhona and San Francisco's Tcho. Though they are a mere fraction of the size of the big three, they are well respected for the quality of their chocolate product, which can cost more than ten dollars a pound. Valrhona and Tcho produce chocolate that goes into handmade, high-end con-

THE THREE YOU'VE NEVER HEARD OF

The three biggest producers of cocoa and chocolate are names you've probably never heard of. That's because they don't sell chocolate to you—they sell chocolate to the people and companies that make products out of chocolate.

These three companies control nearly half of all the cocoa that is harvested and chocolate that is produced in the world. They are Switzerland's Barry Callebaut, Singapore's Olam International, and Cargill, headquartered in the United States. Callebaut alone controls 25 percent of the market, buying up a million tons of cocoa beans every year and processing them in fifty different factories. It makes $5 billion a year from its bean business.

Companies like Nestlé, Mars, Cadbury, and Hershey are big enough to control their own supply of beans. They are called bean-to-bar companies because they buy the actual cocoa beans and go through the entire manufacturing process, all the way to the chocolate you buy at the store. However, they don't process beans in the amounts that Callebaut, Cargill, and Olam do. These three handle more raw cocoa, because they provide the cocoa to the thousands of huge bakeries, candy makers, restaurants, dessert makers, and food manufacturers that use chocolate in some form in their products. Somebody has to sell the chocolate flavoring to the ice-cream makers, the chocolate mix for your local fast-food chocolate milkshake, cocoa for the chocolate birthday cakes made by your local bakery, chocolate frosting for the glazed doughnuts at your local doughnut shop, or icing for the small cookies your local caterer is creating for a wedding party. That's what the big three do.

fections. You would never find this chocolate in, for example, the chocolate cupcakes your local supermarket sells.

While the International Cocoa Organization's list of nine hundred makers seems large, it contains only a small number of the businesses working with chocolate today. It does not include the thousands of small chocolate makers who produce limited amounts of chocolate or craft their own brand of chocolates by hand in small shops. No one knows exactly how many companies around the world make chocolate products. If you add up all the chocolatiers, bakeries, ice-cream shops, doughnut shops, dessert makers, restaurants, and all the other stores that make and sell edible chocolate, you would likely have hundreds of thousands of different places that serve up chocolate concoctions.

Some of the smaller shops make chocolates exactly as they were made a hundred years ago. Many of them are premium chocolatiers who charge more than a few dollars for each individual truffle or small bar, which is significantly more than it costs to buy a Milky Way. But the purity and processing of the chocolate on such a small, personal scale make it worth the money.

You might be familiar with premium chocolate through brands like Godiva and Ethel M. Godiva was started in Belgium in 1926, but has since become a huge company with more than five hundred stores. It is currently part of the Turkish company Yildiz, although for a long time it was owned by Campbell Soup Company. Ethel M is actually a company started by Forrest Mars, and named after his mother. (He included the middle initial "M" in Ethel M so that no one would confuse the company's namesake with his stepmother, who was Ethel V.) Ethel M chocolates are made in Nevada and are popular mail-order gourmet chocolates. You'd never guess that such a high-end product was owned and run by Mars, Inc.—the same company that produces Snickers bars.

Chocolates come in nearly every shape and flavor you can imagine.

WOMEN IN CHOCOLATE

The story of chocolate over the last two centuries was populated primarily by successful businessmen who had the money to invest in buying chocolate-making equipment, or fathers and sons who toiled away trying to create better types of chocolate. Women weren't part of the story, since they were excluded from most businesses in the 1800s and early 1900s. Yet they were there. After all, Frank Mars's mother taught him how to dip chocolate, and H. B. Reese's wife was his partner in the kitchen that produced the first of the fabled Reese's peanut butter cups.

Modern times have wrought a big change in the who's who of the chocolate world. Some of the most delicious and unique chocolate being made today is the product of women with tasty ideas and strong business skills. A perfect example is Vosges Haut-Chocolat, a Chicago-based maker of high-end chocolate bars. It was started by Katrina Markoff, an American who went to culinary school in Paris. She started her own chocolate company in her kitchen in 1998, naming it after a historical section of Paris called Place de Vosges. Her bars featured an astounding array of ingredients mixed into the chocolate, ranging from pink Himalayan crystal salt and chipotle to coconut, curry, wasabi, and bacon.

In the years since, Vosges has opened shops all over America and Markoff has received accolades and awards as a distinguished entrepreneur and developer of extraordinary chocolates. Another woman who has changed the perception about those who make chocolate is Italian chocolatier Cecilia Tessieri. In 1990, Cecilia started a business making handmade European praline candies, which are sugar-and-nut mixtures coated with chocolate. She discovered that the chocolate she bought didn't

Katrina Markoff is one of the pioneers of modern chocolate making, adding exotic and unusual ingredients like curry and bacon to her Vosges bars.

Italian chocolatier Cecilia Tessieri, the founder of Amedei, is know for prize-winning chocolates and her commitment to using the highest quality cocoa beans.

match the quality she wanted. She set out to create her own blend of chocolate so that it would always be exactly what she wanted. Over the next seven years, she researched—and searched for—the perfect combination of beans. Along the way, Tessieri apprenticed with chocolate makers all over Europe and became one of the world's most knowledgeable women on crafting chocolate directly from beans. In 1998, she founded Amedei, a chocolate company named after her grandmother, who had encouraged her to pursue her dream. Tessieri's chocolates have gone on to win international awards and she is recognized in Europe as the first woman to be considered a master chocolatier.

A completely different approach to chocolate has been taken by Maricel Presilla. She was born in Cuba, where her father's family owned cocoa plantations. She arrived in the United States as a teenager and developed a fascination with the various food cultures of Latin America as well as Spanish history. In college she became a culinary historian, exploring how different cultures developed their styles of cooking and how they used different ingredients to develop food. She has written several cookbooks, notably one on chocolate, and is now a recognized authority on how the cocoa tree and its beans have been used over the centuries. Presilla has also opened several restaurants in Hoboken, New Jersey. While she's not in the business of making chocolate bars, she is demonstrating how versatile cocoa and chocolate can be in every type of cooking, from breakfast to dessert.

Just as the chocolate business is far different from what it was a hundred years ago, so too are the types of people who are creating chocolate. As chocolate evolves into ever more tantalizing forms, women are already among the leaders in exploring new ways to concoct the world's favorite confection.

More and more gourmet chocolates are being crafted by trained chocolatiers who run tiny shops. Today's chocolatiers are usually educated at culinary school or apprenticed to a master. For those who go to culinary school, it is similar to going to college and then getting an advanced degree. At least four years are spent learning everything there is to know about chocolate. It is worth noting that in parts of Europe, culinary programs have the same status as universities known for exceptional academic or sports programs. They are extremely competitive and require their students to become highly skilled in whatever they are studying.

A chocolatier's education begins with learning about the different types of cocoa beans and understanding their subtle differences. The chocolatier is taught the chemistry of cocoa and chocolate: how it changes when mixed with other ingredients, and how it is affected by temperature and time. Among the most important lessons is how to change the flavor and texture of chocolate using this knowledge of chemistry.

Once the chocolatier understands all the elements of what chocolate is, their training turns to working with chocolate itself. The chocolatier learns how to select different types of chocolate for specific concoctions, such as bonbons, bars, and truffles. The mixture of ingredients—whether it be spices, fruits, nuts, etc.—ultimately contributes to how the chocolatier develops a signature style of their own. Pouring and molding chocolate, as well as shaping it, comes next.

Finally, the chocolatier learns about designing chocolate in a visual way, with a focus on making it attractive to look at, and learning about presentation—how to arrange it for maximum appeal to the person who will be eating it. This means not only creating an interesting shape, size, or design for the chocolate itself, but also how to display the chocolate on a plate, alongside other food, or in a shop.

When their education is complete, many chocolatiers go to work in bakeries (known in Europe as patisseries) or restaurants. There they work day in and day out to create everything from chocolate croissants for breakfast to

Left: A chocolatier pours chocolate on a slab in preparation for molding.

Below: Fine chocolates are designed to look almost as good as they taste.

chocolate mousse desserts for dinners.

Some go on to open their own shops. An excellent example is Vincent Koenig, who runs a small chocolate shop and French bakery outside of New York City in Fairfield, Connecticut. Called Isabelle et Vincent, it is run by Vincent and his wife. Their two children work in the shop, which is located in a refurbished house in the town center.

Vincent is a seventh-generation chef—and a third-generation chocolatier—who was born in France. He grew up in Strasbourg, a town that lies on the border of France, Switzerland, and Germany, and learned his craft from his father and grandfather. Vincent then went to the famous Chambre de Métiers d'Alsace culinary school in France. After several years of work and study, he received a master's degree in culinary skills. Upon completing his final exam, he was recognized by the culinary school as a Master Chocolatier, someone who is certified as being an expert in all things chocolate.

He opened a shop in Strasbourg, and soon his chocolates were renowned in France. He and Isabelle ran their shop and sold his award-winning creations for eighteen years before deciding to move to the United States. They wanted their children to receive an American education, and they thought it would be an exceptional country in which to grow a business (although their friends told them that Americans weren't ready for high-end chocolates like Vincent's).

The Koenigs opened their Connecticut shop in 2008, just as Americans were starting to think of chocolate as more than just wrapped bars from Mars or Nestlé. Vincent brought his own recipes with him from France along with all his own chocolate-making equipment.

Isabelle and Vincent Koenig in their Connecticut store.

As soon as he and Isabelle opened their store, people started lining up for Vincent's chocolates. At first it might have been the novelty of it all, but eventually people realized that Vincent's chocolate was a completely different food experience from the candy they were buying in the checkout lines at grocery stores. He specializes in small solid chocolates as well as candied lemon and orange strips dipped in chocolate. Vincent's dark chocolate is 72 percent cocoa, while his milk chocolate is 38 percent (milk chocolate bars you get in the grocery are only about 10 percent cocoa). In addition, he creates baked goods that have chocolate threaded through and around them, like mousse cake, chocolate-dipped cookies, and éclairs.

Vincent's business is very much like his grandfather's was a century ago. He gets to his shop by three a.m. every day to start the ovens for bread and the melters for chocolate. Then he decides which variety of his chocolates to make that day. Part of the decision is determined by the time of year and if there are any holidays coming up on the calendar. (On the days before Easter and Christmas, he makes triple the amount of candy of a normal day.)

Once he has decided, Vincent lays out the ingredients in an open cooking area that is about the size of a regular kitchen—during business hours, customers can see the process happening behind the counter. The area is spotless and has no wasted space. Almost every ingredient and machine is reachable with a single step.

He buys his chocolate from Guittard, a California chocolate company that sells some of the highest quality chocolate in the world to chocolatiers and chefs. The beans Guittard uses are selected from only a few plantations in the world. Vincent has also used Valrhona, which is considered one of Europe's finest cocoa providers. He buys more than several hundred pounds of chocolate a month—more than two tons every year. Every hundred pounds will translate into about three hundred pounds of finished product once he has added all his other ingredients.

Vincent's equipment consists of two stirring vats, a melter, many molds and a storage rack for molds, and a huge marble table to lay the chocolates out on.

Starting with the melter, Vincent heats the bars until they become a thick liquid. When he's satisfied with the texture and taste, he begins the process of mixing the liquid chocolate with ingredients and pouring it into molds. He keeps the entire area at 68 degrees Fahrenheit to make sure everything stays fresh.

As he ladles chocolate into the molds, he quickly adds the elements that make the chocolates uniquely his: a dash of pralines, some salt, a sliver of fruit. Once the molds are filled, they are set aside to cool. Vincent allows his chocolate to sit untouched for twenty-four hours in order to reach the perfect temperature before he removes it from the molds.

After a full day of cooling, the chocolates are then placed on trays and taken to the front of the store. Isabelle arranges them in the shop's display cases next to a wide variety of breads and pastries. By that time, people are already lined up to start buying the unique chocolate that Vincent has created.

For all the sweet side of the job, the Koenigs work incredibly hard. Their store is open seven days a week, and Vincent spends fourteen to eighteen hours in the kitchen every day, getting barely five hours of sleep a night. But it is what he loves doing, and he's become successful by being so good at what he does.

In Norwalk, Connecticut, just a few miles from Isabelle et Vincent, is a chocolate shop and café called Chocopologie. Run by Danish chocolatier Fritz Knipschildt, it features high-end chocolates, including the world's single most expensive piece of chocolate. It is called La Madeline au Truffe, and features Valrhona dark chocolate surrounding an actual truffle. While chocolate truffles are bite-size balls of hard chocolate around a soft chocolate center, "real" truffles are a type of mushroom (technically, a fungus) found only in certain parts of France. (They are rooted out by trained pigs and dogs who scour the forests for them.) These forest truffles are considered the most expensive food in the world. So Knipschildt has placed an actual truffle inside a chocolate truffle . . . and each piece costs $250.00. Despite how bizarre it sounds, it is supposedly a tremendous-tasting chocolate.

Inventive chocolatiers are using ingredients like salt, wasabi, olives, habaneros, pink peppercorn, and passion fruit to create entirely new taste sensations.

Like the Koenigs and Fritz Knipschildt, there are many families and chocolatiers all over the United States—and the world—working to build their own chocolate businesses. A lot of them are not only skilled artisans but people seeking to make changes in the chocolate business. Many of them only buy organically grown chocolate, or chocolate that is certified as having come from plantations that don't use slave labor. They're also changing the way we think of chocolate by using less sugar and filler and higher percentages of actual cocoa. They are promoting chocolate as a good and enjoyable food—not a junk food.

It's possible that one of these people will be the next Milton Hershey or John Cadbury. Until then, you should look for a local chocolatier and try at least one of their offerings. It might make you want to head to chocolate school yourself.

THE NOT-SO-SWEET SIDE OF CHOCOLATE

More than 70 percent of the world's cocoa beans come from West Africa. It is estimated that there are two million small plantations in that part of the continent, most of those owned by families or small businesses. The average size of these plantations is roughly five acres, or the equivalent of four football fields. By comparison, the average American farm is more than four hundred acres.

Growing cocoa is one of the most important sources of income for millions of people in Africa. Cocoa-related jobs range from tending to the trees and harvesting the cocoa pods to drying the beans and packing and transporting them for sale. Many of the world's chocolate makers rely on these plantations and their workers to provide them with a nonstop supply of cocoa. If it weren't for the work these people do, you wouldn't be able to stop by your local store to pick up a chocolate bar anytime you wanted.

That's the positive side of cocoa growing. There is, unfortunately, a downside. The vast majority of people who work harvesting cocoa in Africa have never tasted chocolate. The beans they pick are packed up and shipped to other continents for processing. The large chocolate manufacturers don't send much chocolate product back to Africa, because most of the population is too poor to afford it. Not only have these people not tasted chocolate, they've rarely even seen it—even though their livelihood is based on the rest of the world wanting ever-increasing amounts of chocolate.

There is yet a more sinister side to the cocoa business in Africa. Growing cocoa trees is a business, and some African plantation owners will do anything to make sure they get as much money from their cocoa as they can—even if they have to break the law to do it. Despite the fact that cocoa is a big business around the world, and chocolate gets ever more expensive the closer it gets to the store, plantation owners don't make a lot of money from their crops. In order to gain the most value out of their plantations, owners have to try to harvest every single pod on every single tree. This is hard work, as it involves cutting the pods off trees with machetes and then carrying them in large sacks back to a sorting area. The pods have to be harvested within a specific period of time, or they will rot.

Workers splitting cocoa pods by hand on an African cocoa plantation.

Plantation owners need a lot of help to make sure the pods are completely collected. Many rely on family members. Others hire workers to come and work during the harvest. And still others—who don't want to pay their workers—use slaves to pick their pods. Sometimes, those slaves are children.

There have been many documented reports in recent years of slave labor being used on cocoa plantations. Much as they were on American cotton and tobacco plantations during the 1700s and 1800s, the slaves are considered cheap or free labor by the owners. They get nothing more than food and a place to live, with no pay and no way to leave. In America, slaves were taken from Africa and shipped across the ocean. In today's African plantations, the slaves are smuggled in from surrounding countries, towns, and villages.

Smugglers kidnap young children from countries such as Mali and Burkina Faso and sell them to plantation owners in cocoa-growing countries such as Cote d'Ivoire and Ghana. Sometimes the children are taken when their parents aren't around. Other times, they are lured with the promise of making lots of money. Sometimes, their parents even sell them. In every case, the children are sent to do dangerous work in the cocoa fields with no pay.

Since the late 1990s, attempts have been made by both governments and large chocolate companies to stop the use of slaves and children in cocoa plantations. The United States and other countries signed an agreement in 2001—known as the Cocoa Protocol—wherein they pledged to cooperate in ending slave labor. Many of the chocolate companies have stated that they won't buy beans from plantations that use child or slave labor. However, they also claim that they can't check on whether every person who works on a cocoa plantation is of legal age to work or is being paid for their work.

While the amount of abusive child labor and slavery appears to have been reduced in recent years, it has not disappeared. Human rights groups have demanded that the chocolate companies become more actively involved in making sure that plantation owners are using legitimate workers. These same groups also want the chocolate companies to pay a bit more for cocoa beans so that plantation owners will have more money to pay their workers—which could potentially convince them not to resort to slaves.

There are a number of organizations working on making the harvesting of cocoa a better practice. Fair Trade USA, Equal Exchange, Fairtrade International, and the Rainforest Alliance all have programs specifically for the cocoa industry. Some provide certifications to chocolate makers that prove they've done their best to pay a fair amount for cocoa and acquire it from plantations with proper working environments. Chocolate products that meet the standards of these organizations often have a "Fair Trade" label on them.

14

CHOCOHOLICS AND COCOA CULTURE

CHOCOLATE ISN'T JUST SOMETHING WE PUT IN our mouths and give as gifts. It has become a part of our culture in many ways, some of them quite unusual. And for everyone in the United States today, chocolate is part of their history.

Chocolate's early days as a bitter drink for wealthy people are long behind it.

The colonies were importing chocolate by the late 1600s. In the years leading up to the Revolutionary War, Benjamin Franklin sold chocolate in his print shop. In 1785 Thomas Jefferson wrote a letter to John Adams, professing his admiration of chocolate: "By getting it good in quality, and cheap in price, the superiority of the article both for health and nourishment will soon give it the same preference over tea and coffee in America."

Cocoa and chocolate went beyond stores and kitchens to become essential parts of world exploration during the early 1900s. Explorers like Ernest Shackleton and Robert Scott, who sought to chart the mysteries of the Arctic and Antarctic, took British cocoa with them on their expeditions. On his quest to be the first person to reach the South Pole in 1911, Roald Amundsen ensured that his men had at least a quarter pound of cocoa or chocolate every day to keep up their strength. Richard E. Byrd carried Nestlé chocolate and cocoa powder on his famous North and South Pole expeditions.

In 1953, Sir Edmund Hillary and Tenzing Norgay became the first people to reach the top of Mount Everest, at 29,035 feet the tallest mountain in the world. When packing the supplies for their dangerous trek, they included chocolate bars and cocoa to provide nourishment and energy. All told, the journey, from establishing their base camp in Nepal to completing the climb, took two months. When they reached the summit, Norgay—who had lived in the shadow of Everest his entire life—buried a bar of chocolate in the snow as an offering to the gods of the mountain.

From the food kits of adventurers traveling the world to snacks at lunchtime, chocolate has seemingly reached into every single element of modern life over the past century.

Explorers have packed chocolate in their packs as a source of energy—and as a gift to the gods.

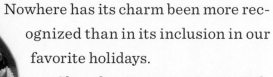

Nowhere has its charm been more recognized than in its inclusion in our favorite holidays.

Chocolate's connection to Valentine's Day is the most obvious. In its earliest days, chocolate was an expensive and rare food. It was regarded as something reserved for the rich and the royal. So on those occasions when it was given as a gift by regular people, it denoted a sacrifice—and hence, a great deal of affection. Valentine's Day was the day on which this affection was most publicly shown.

As for all those heart-shaped boxes filled with chocolates, it is believed that the Cadbury company had a hand in that. When John Cadbury retired in 1861, his sons Richard and George took over. Richard was a skilled painter, and took to designing unusual and arty chocolate boxes in which to sell the company's chocolates to help with sales. He believed that if the boxes were made pretty and functional, they would also be used to store small items after the chocolates were gone—keeping the Cadbury name around, even if the chocolates weren't.

Sometime in the late 1860s, he crafted a heart-shaped box to package the company's chocolates. History doesn't record whether or not Richard did this specifically for Valentine's Day, but the boxes became favorites among Cadbury customers during the month of February. Other chocolate makers followed suit, creating boxes similar to those made by Richard. Today there

Holidays all around the world have become occasions to give chocolate as gifts.

are dozens upon dozens of heart-shaped boxes of chocolates to choose from every February 14.

Richard Cadbury may have also been partially responsible for all the chocolate eggs on the shelves at Easter. The notion of chicken eggs being used at Easter came from the seasonal birth of many animals during the spring, which coincided with the annual Easter feast. People throughout Europe took to creating elaborate egg-shaped objects to celebrate the season, making them out of everything from dough to diamonds. The famous Fabergé eggs, created in Russia during the 1800s, were made of gold and precious stones for Czar Alexander III, who gave them to his wife as Easter presents. They have come to be valued as priceless pieces of art.

With just about everything of value being shaped into eggs, it's no surprise that chocolate was also shaped into ovoids (that's the technical term for "egg-shaped things"). In the early 1800s, confectioners in France and Germany started to mold soft chocolate into eggs. They used the same bitter chocolate used for making the cocoa drink, so we're not sure if people used the eggs as an interesting shape for preparing the beverage or whether they might have tried to gnaw on them as well.

When Richard and George Cadbury took over their father's company, chocolate had barely become an "edible" passion. The rival Fry company had introduced the first chocolate bars for eating barely fourteen years earlier, and those were hard, bitter slabs. But the Cadbury brothers were innovators. As soon

Many of the world's candy makers have crafted egg-shaped chocolates, from Cadbury Creme Eggs to Reese's Peanut Butter Egg.

as they were able to pour liquid chocolate into molds in their factory, they created ovoid molds. They introduced dark-chocolate eggs in 1875, just in time for Easter. Richard oversaw the decoration of the eggs, which featured designs on the outside of the molded chocolate.

After Cadbury's introduction of the Dairy Milk bar in 1905 proved that milk chocolate appealed to nearly everyone who ate it, Cadbury started making milk chocolate versions of its eggs. These were followed by hollow eggs, as well as eggs with sugar creme inside them, which were introduced in 1923. Cadbury Creme Eggs, which have evolved over the last ninety years, are now the biggest-selling chocolate item throughout Britain between New Year's Day and Easter. The company makes more than five hundred million every year.

No discussion of chocolate and holidays is complete without Halloween. This holiday came about as the opposite of Easter. Even though the name comes from "All Hallows' Eve," which signified the night before the Christian holiday of All Saints' Day, it was originally a holiday to celebrate the end of the harvest. This was a time when the fields were cleared, animals started preparing for hibernation or migration, and winter was on the way. It all signaled the temporary "death" of nature—just as spring celebrated nature's rebirth. Christian tradition also chose this exact same time of the year to honor the souls of those who had died. Halloween and its ghoulish and ghostly rites thus both celebrated the change of seasons and marked the remembrance of the dead.

Today's Halloween is a combination of rituals and pageants from many different countries. Going from house to house came from the Irish practice of celebrating the end of the harvest by visiting neighbors with lanterns carved from gourds or pumpkins. One legend has it that since it was dark at that time of the year, people wore disguises so that demons that haunted the night wouldn't recognize them—or try to trick them. Throw in lots of other historical celebrations from all over the world, and we get the tradition of dressing up for Halloween and going from house to house to seek treats and possibly play some tricks.

Celebrating during All Hallows' Eve has been going on for hundreds of years. But candy at Halloween? That's pretty new, barely sixty years old. Up until the late 1940s—just after World War II—Halloween wasn't even recognized as any kind of official holiday. It was optional; some people celebrated, some didn't. When kids went to different houses in their costumes, they were likely to get whatever the homeowners had lying around. That could be pennies, candied apples, bags of nuts, cupcakes, oranges, or whatever was cheap and easy to give. (Candied apples, while one of the sweeter offerings, often gunked up all the other items in the bag.) Sometimes it would be gumballs or lollipops, and occasionally Hershey's bars.

As chocolate became cheaper in the 1950s and 1960s, people started buying chocolate bars for Halloween. They were easy to hand out—no mess—and kids always liked them. Plus, as Halloween gained popularity and a steadily increasing number of kids showed up year after year, candy was a cheap way to deal with all the trick-or-treaters.

The real switch to "all candy all the time" came in the late 1960s and early 1970s. News stories around the country at the time featured Halloween horrors that involved razor blades in apples or poison found in homemade cupcakes and unwrapped penny candy. Suddenly Halloween was dangerous. It became a concern every year, with warnings on TV and in schools. Parents threw out anything in their kids' bags that wasn't wrapped and protectively sealed. No more apples, no more cupcakes, no more gumballs. The safe alternative was wrapped candy, a huge percentage of which were Hershey's Kisses, Snickers, Milky Ways, Baby Ruths, and other sealed chocolates.

Sales of chocolate skyrocket in the weeks leading up to Halloween.

In response to the demand, Hershey, Mars, and the other big chocolate makers began selling small giveaway sizes of their most popular products. These could be purchased in big bags and were perfect for handing out to every kid who rang the bell. By the end of the 1970s, wrapped candy was the only reliable, parent-approved treat for Halloween.

Looking back on the dangerous-treats scare nearly fifty years later, it turns out that it was all over nothing. In reality, there was not a single case of hazardous Halloween treats being handed out. Not one. The stories had all been rumors that had spread from town to town and were picked up and reported as fact by the news media. The razor blades and poison never happened. Of course, that's beside the point. Wrapped chocolate now symbolizes Halloween as much as masks and costumes do. Nothing else will do for the millions of kids who go out in search of free treats every October 31.

In retrospect, the scare was one of the best things that ever happened to the chocolate business. It meant guaranteed sales of millions of pieces of candy during a formerly slow period for chocolate purchases. Some people even believe that the whole scare might have been part of a conspiracy by the chocolate companies themselves—that chocolate executives started the rumors of poisoned fruit to convince people that their wrapped products were the only safe option at Halloween. It makes for an evil story of corporate bad guys that ties in nicely with the creepiness of Halloween, but no one has ever proven that it's true.

Since we're on the subject of creepy things, chocolate had a starring role in one of the creepiest films of all time, *Psycho*. Considered one of the best horror movies ever made, it was directed by Alfred Hitchcock in 1960.

Even though color film was available, Hitchcock chose to film the movie in black-and-white to make *Psycho* look scarier. During filming, he laid out a scene where blood would be flowing down a bathtub drain. It was a dramatic part of the movie, but none of the fake Hollywood blood—usually red food coloring mixed with corn syrup—looked right in black-and-white. After trying various liquids, Hitchcock hit on one that looked perfect: chocolate syrup. It had the

Alfred Hitchcock was a master at creating scary movies. He found that chocolate syrup looked like blood when it was photographed in black and white.

right amount of shine and dripped exactly as blood did. The onscreen blood was reportedly Bosco's syrup, and not Hershey's.

Hershey, however, got a lead role in the 1982 movie *E.T. the Extra-Terrestrial*, about an alien stranded on Earth that is trying to find its way home. One of the movie's plot points had the story's hero, ten-year-old Elliott, trying to lure the frightened E.T. to his house using a path made of candy. The script called for Elliott to use M&M's.

Director Steven Spielberg and his team approached the executives at Mars, Inc. about using M&M's and possibly having Mars help to promote the movie. However, Mars, Inc.—run at that time by Forrest's two sons—decided they didn't want anything to do with it. While the reason has never been fully revealed, it's believed that Mars, Inc. found the E.T. character so odd-looking and the movie's plot so weird that they felt their brand would be damaged by being part of it.

So the filmmakers went to Hershey, which was selling a relatively new product called Reese's Pieces. Like M&M's, except filled with peanut butter, Reese's Pieces looked very similar to M&M's. Because they had been introduced to the market only a little more than a year earlier, Reese's Pieces weren't well-known by consumers. Hershey agreed to work with the *E.T.* team to not only provide the candy but also do product tie-ins and advertising. This meant

Reese's Pieces became popular as soon as the character of E.T. was seen to be eating them.

that Hershey would help pay for some of the movie's publicity in return for getting to use the image of E.T. on its Reese's products and in its advertising.

The week that the movie came out, sales of Reese's Pieces tripled. Many retailers sold out all their candy within days of the movie's opening. Movie houses all over America added the candy to their concession stands, right next to the popcorn. Reese's Pieces went on to become one of Hershey's most popular products, and *E.T.* went on to become one of the most popular movies in history.

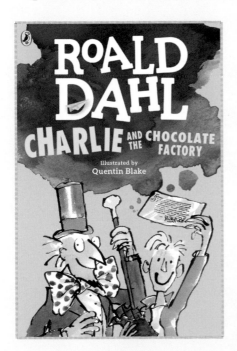

Roald Dahl's story of a magical chocolate factory has entertained generations of readers and inspired two movies.

Chocolate itself has been the subject of several movies, the best known being *Willy Wonka and the Chocolate Factory*. To this day, Willy Wonka is sort of chocolate's Wizard of Oz. People have used Wonka's Chocolate Factory as an example of the wonders of chocolate making since the original movie came out in 1971.

Based on Roald Dahl's 1964 children's book *Charlie and the Chocolate Factory*, the movie was actually produced as a way to promote a candy bar that didn't even exist yet. Quaker Oats, best known as the company that makes breakfast food and granola bars, was looking to create a brand of candies in 1970. It met with some Hollywood producers, who suggested using Dahl's book as the basis for a film that could feature Quaker Oats' new products.

Quaker Oats loved the idea so much that it funded the making of the entire movie. The company even decided to name its new candy the "Wonka Bar," and got Roald Dahl's permission to use the name. The Wonka Bar would appear in the film, and, to make the connection even more obvious, the title character of the film would be changed from Charlie to Willy Wonka—which is why the movie has a different name from the book.

Years later Quaker Oats got out of the candy business and sold the Wonka brand to Nestlé.

In 2005, Johnny Depp starred in another cinematic version of Dahl's book, which this time kept the original title. Coincidentally, Depp also starred in a movie called *Chocolat*, about a small chocolate shop in France that changes the lives of everyone who enters it.

Chocolate might not actually change the lives of everyone who eats it, but there is a strange statistic that eating chocolate might help produce Nobel Prize winners. In 2012, the *New England Journal of Medicine*, one of the world's most respected medical publications, showed that countries with the highest consumption of chocolate also had the most Nobel Prize winners (relative to the size of their population).

The report suggested that the flavonols in chocolate might affect the brain, and people who eat more of it might think "bigger" than others.

Regardless of its benefits to our brains, chocolate is eaten because it tastes good. For many people, who like to call themselves chocoholics, it is their favorite food. Those who truly love chocolate can never get enough and are always looking for more extreme chocolate experiences. Bakeries and ice-cream shops regularly offer products to appeal to those who like their chocolate intense, thick, and rich. Doubling or tripling up on the amount of cocoa or chocolate flavor leads to food with humorous names like "Death by Chocolate" or "Chocolate Murder." This is supposed to be chocolate so intense that it's worth dying for (not literally, but you get the idea).

To keep chocolate lovers happy, every U.S. state and most countries have annual chocolate fairs and festivals, featuring chocolate in every imaginable

CHOCOLATE CONSUMPTION
VS
NOBEL PRIZE WINNERS

POUNDS OF CHOCOLATE CONSUMED PER PERSON EVERY YEAR

26 lbs · 14 lbs · 19 lbs · 17 lbs · 21 lbs · 11 lbs

32 · 31 · 25 · 24 · 23 · 10

NOBEL PRIZE WINNERS PER 10 MILLION PEOPLE

Research has found that countries where people eat a lot of chocolate also produce a lot of Nobel Prize winners.

size, shape, and form—from handmade chocolates to chocolate sculptures and chocolate-making competitions. These events are attended by millions of people every year.

In short, chocolate has come a long way from being the drink prized by the Aztecs and kept secret by the royalty of Europe. Just about anyone who wants chocolate can get it at a nearby store. Thanks to the tinkering of hundreds of men and women over the past hundred years, chocolate has become the world's most popular flavor and the world's favorite type of candy. While at one time it might have been the exotic and elite "food of the gods," today it is the popular and enchanting "food of everyone."

MOST POPULAR CHOCOLATE BRANDS
IN THE UNITED STATES IN 2015

1. **m&m's**
2. **Reese's** PEANUT BUTTER CUPS
3. **SNICKERS**
4. **HERSHEY'S** Milk Chocolate
5. **Kit Kat**
6. **Twix**
7. **3 Musketeers**
8. **HERSHEY'S** Cookies 'n' Creme
9. **Milky Way**
10. **Almond Joy**

GLOSSARY

◆◆◆◆◆◆◆◆◆◆◆◆◆◆◆◆◆◆◆◆◆◆◆◆

BLOOM: Visible blotchiness or white patches that occur in chocolate when it has too much moisture or has been tempered and cooled at the wrong temperature.

CACAO: The Spanish interpretation of the Aztecs' word for the native plant and drink, which sounded like "kaw-kaw." It is usually interchangeable with "cocoa." Many people and companies have taken to using the term to identify all the parts of the plant and its products up until cocoa powder is produced. This means cacao tree, cacao pods, cacao beans, cacao nibs, and cacao solids.

COCOA: A name for chocolate and various forms of chocolate, as well as many of the elements that go into the creation of chocolate. Cocoa—interchangeable with cacao—is also the name given to the tree, pod, bean, nibs, solids, powder, and related products that are necessary to create chocolate. In addition, it is the name for the drink that has evolved from the first known use of the crushed cocoa beans.

COCOA BEAN: Seeds of the cocoa tree. The beans are found inside pods that grow on the trunk of the tree, and there are several dozen seeds per pod.

COCOA BUTTER: The oily fat in the cocoa bean. It is initially separated from cocoa solids during grinding. Additional squeezing of the beans releases more cocoa butter. It is creamy and pourable when in liquid form, almost solid when cool.

COCOA CAKE: A dry cocoa mass that remains after the cocoa butter is squeezed out of the nibs. Also called a press cake. This cake is broken up into cocoa powder.

COCOA CRUMB: A dry mixture of cocoa powder and sugar and milk solids. Cocoa butter is added into this mix to make milk chocolate.

COCOA LIQUOR: Another term for cocoa mass.

COCOA MASS: A paste that results from grinding cocoa beans down into a mixture of cocoa butter and cocoa solids.

COCOA POD: The seed casing that grows from the bark of the cocoa tree. Each tree grows about thirty mature pods a season, and each pod grows to the size of a football.

COCOA POWDER: A fine, dry powder made from sifting the cocoa cake. This is used for making chocolate.

COCOA SOLIDS: What remains of the cocoa after all the cocoa butter is pressed out. The dry cocoa cake is made up of cocoa solids.

COCOA TREE: The plant from which cocoa pods and their seeds are harvested. The tree is delicate and grows naturally only in a narrow geographical band 20 degrees above and below the equator.

CONCHING: The constant stirring, moving, and rotating of cocoa butter and cocoa powder inside specialized machines to create a smooth texture before the chocolate is tempered. It removes grittiness and improves flavor and lasts anywhere from several hours to several days.

CRIOLLO: The rarest and most prized of the three types of cocoa tree. Pronounced "cree-oh-yo."

DARK CHOCOLATE: Chocolate products that are at least 35 percent cocoa solids (meaning a maximum of 65 percent cocoa butter and other additives).

DUTCH CHOCOLATE / DUTCH PROCESS: Chocolate that has alkali salts added to it to reduce bitterness and acidity. This process makes the chocolate nearly black.

FERMENTATION: A process in which cocoa beans are removed from their pods and left to soak in the juice from the pod pulp. This infuses the beans with flavor before they are dried and cracked open.

FORASTERO: The hardiest and most common of the three primary types of cocoa plant. More than three-quarters of all cocoa beans come from Forastero trees, most of which are in Africa.

GRINDERS: Heavy weights or machines that crush the cocoa butter out of nibs.

MILK CHOCOLATE: Processed chocolate that has milk and sugar added to it. The milk is typically added as a powder or a solid. Because of the addition of milk and sugar, milk chocolate usually contains less than 30 percent cocoa solids.

NIBS: The heart of the cocoa bean after it has been fermented, dried, cracked, and winnowed. Cocoa solids and cocoa butter come from the crushed nibs.

ROASTING: The method of increasing the flavor of cocoa beans by heating them, which also dries out the shells so they can be cracked and removed.

TEMPERING: The precise process of heating and then cooling chocolate in the last stages of its production.

TRINITARIO: A hybrid of Criollo and Forastero trees, resulting in a third strain of cocoa plant. It is hardier than Criollo and fruitier tasting than Forastero. Trinitario beans make up just over 10 percent of all chocolate products.

WHITE CHOCOLATE: Raw cocoa butter mixed with sugar and milk. It has no cocoa powder or solids in it, which means that it is not technically a form of chocolate.

WINNOWING: The process of removing all shells and shell fragments from cocoa nibs. This is done using screens, sieves, jets of air, and vacuuming devices after the shells are cracked.

SOURCES

◆◆◆◆◆◆◆◆◆◆◆◆◆◆◆◆◆◆◆◆◆◆

Brenner, Joël Glenn. *The Emperors of Chocolate: Inside the Secret World of Hershey and Mars.* New York: Random House, 1998.

Bugbee, James McKellar, and Walter Baker & Company. *Cocoa and Chocolate: A Short History of Their Production and Use.* Dorchester, Mass.: Walter Baker & Company, 1907.

Cadbury, Deborah. *Chocolate Wars: The 150-Year Rivalry Between the World's Greatest Chocolate Makers.* New York: Public Affairs, 2010.

Grivetti, Louis Evan, and Howard-Yana Shapiro, eds. *Chocolate: History, Culture, and Heritage.* Hoboken, N.J.: John Wiley & Sons, 2009.

Mercier, Jacques. *The Temptation of Chocolate.* Tielt, Belgium: Lannoo Publishers, 2008.

Mistrati, Miki. *The Dark Side of Chocolate.* DVD. Directed by Miki Mistrati and U. Roberto Romano. Bastard Film, 2010.

STATISTICS AND SALES NUMBERS

Candy Industry Magazine: http://www.candyindustry.com

Confectionery News: http://www.confectionerynews.com

Directive 2000/36/EC of the European Parliament and of the Council of 23 June 2000 relating to cocoa and chocolate products intended for human consumption: http://eur-lex.europa.eu/LexUriServ/LexUriServ. do?uri=CELEX:32000L0036:EN:NOT

RELATING TO SUGAR AND USE IN U.S. CHOCOLATE

http://worldcocoafoundation.org/wp-content/uploads/Economic_Profile_of_the_US_ Chocolate_Industry_2011.pdf

Euromonitor International: http://www.euromonitor.com

OTHER CHOCOLATE RESOURCES

Scientific, Agricultural, and Organizational Websites and Further Research

American Chemical Society: Cooks with Chemistry—The Elements of Chocolate
   workshop: http://acselementsofchocolate.typepad.com

Cornell University Albert R. Mann Library: *Chocolate: Food of the Gods* online exhibit:
   http://exhibits.mannlib.cornell.edu/chocolate/theobromacacao.php

Fair Trade Federation: http://www.fairtradefederation.org

   Fair Trade USA: http://www.fairtradeusa.org

International Cocoa Organization: http://icco.org

Kew Royal Botanic Gardens: http://www.kew.org/plants-fungi/Theobroma-cacao.htm

Museum of Cocoa and Chocolate: http://www.mucc.be/EN/index_en.htm

Rainforest Alliance: http://www.rainforest-alliance.org

World Cocoa Foundation: http://worldcocoafoundation.org

Company Websites

Amedei: http://www.amedei.it

Barry Callebaut: http://barry-callebaut.com

Cadbury: https://www.cadbury.com.au/About-Chocolate.aspx

Cailler: http://cailler.ch/en/recipes

Hans Sloane: http://www.sirhanssloane.com

Hershey: http://www.hersheys.com

Hershey Community Archives: http://www.hersheyarchives.org

Isabelle et Vincent: http://www.isabelleetvincent.com

Madre Chocolate: http://madrechocolate.com/Home.html

Mars: http://www.mars.com/global/brands/chocolate.aspx

Mars Real Chocolate Program: http://www.realchocolate.com

Nestlé: http://www.Nestlé.com/aboutus/history

Original Hawaiian Chocolate: http://www.ohcf.us

Peter's Chocolate: http://www.peterschocolate.com/pages/history.html

Tcho: http://www.tcho.com

Toblerone: http://www.toblerone.co.uk/history/howitbegan/1868

Van Houten: http://www.vanhoutendrinks.com/en/history

Vosges: http://www.vosgeschocolate.com

Wild Ophelia: http://www.wildophelia.com/#our-chocolate

INDEX

◆◆◆◆◆◆◆◆◆◆◆◆◆◆◆◆◆◆◆◆◆◆◆◆◆◆◆◆

Note: Page numbers in **bold** indicate glossary terms. Page numbers in *italics* indicate photographs and illustrations.

ACKNOWLEDGMENTS

◆◆◆◆◆◆◆◆◆◆◆◆◆◆◆◆◆◆◆◆◆◆

If you've read everything to this point, you've learned that making chocolate is an incredibly difficult and complex process that takes lots of time, lots of people, and lots of effort. But the result is truly worth it.

The same is true of writing a book and seeing it through to completion. While it looks like a simple product—as does chocolate—a book involves more than sitting around writing words and then putting pretty pictures around them. It requires research to make sure the history and facts are correct, finding the best photos and illustrations to go with the words, deciding on a visual theme for the book, double-checking facts, moving things around to get them to fit and look right, and then assembling everything to create the book you have in your hands.

The people who were part of that complex process deserve their own thanks. It starts with Alec Shane, who found this book a home before we'd ever met in person. Applause for Nancy Brennan, who did a thoroughly stunning job with layout and images; Janet Pascal, who jumped in midstream to finish blending the thousands of ingredients into a beautiful finished product; Sharyn November, who acquired the book; and Ken Wright, who still finds himself inexplicably linked to most of my books.

I want to acknowledge those people who provided me with insights into the world of chocolate as I traveled around the world: Nat Bletter, who not only shared his love of chocolate and taught me how to make my own, but shared his knowledge of the botanical world of Theobroma. Nat's company, Madre Chocolates, produces some of the finest chocolate in the world, and if you visit Hawaii, take his chocolate-making classes. I am grateful to Pam and Bob Cooper, and Fernando Zamudio, of the Original Hawaiian Chocolate Factory for the tour of their Kona plantation on the island of Hawai'i—and for letting me wander freely about. A nod and a wink to Nguyen Than, who told me and my wife on the shores of the South China Sea that there were two things that Vietnam wasn't good at producing—and chocolate was one of them. (He was right.) A standing ovation for Peter Koppes and his long-distance support, and especially for hand-delivering a carton of fresh Violet Crumbles direct to my house from Australia. Thanks to Isabelle and Vincent Koenig for sharing the details of running a chocolate business, and the shops in Asheville, North Carolina, and Santa Fe, New Mexico, that introduced me to the incredible experience of drinking liquid Mayan and Aztec cocoa. Many of these trips were made possible thanks to my involvement with The National GUITAR Museum and its host venues. Finally, to my great-grandfather Lee Hull Starr, whose Saturday morning trips to the Morris Corner Store always resulted in a chocolate bar—back when they cost less than a quarter.

I'm thankful to be a writer, and to have the support and friendship of people who are interested in what it is I do for a living. That list includes my parents; my brothers and sisters (a special nod to the West Coast Newquists for ongoing Violet Crumble supplies); my nieces and nephews; Michael and Barb Johnson and family, Tucker Greco (RIP) and family, Bill Brahos, Bill Leary, Peter Fitzpatrick, Bill McGuinness, Al Mowrer, Gerard Huerta, David Hill, Rod Hansen and family, Dave and Deb Shlager; writing compatriots Rich Maloof and Pete Prown; and those illustrious teachers who encouraged me decades ago, John Kunkel and Thomas Werge.

Every book I've written is only complete when I mention Trini, Madeline, and Katherine. Their existence has made my life sweeter than a universe of chocolate.

HP Newquist is the author of more than twenty books, including *The Great Brain Book*, a National Science Teachers Association and Children's Book Council Outstanding Science Book, and *The Book of Blood*, an American Association for the Advancement of Science Award finalist. He is also the author of books for the Smithsonian Institution/Viking Innovation and Impact series, including *The Human Body*.

To research this book, Newquist spent time on a cocoa plantation, learned how to make chocolate, and then sampled chocolate from Venice to Vietnam. When not writing or traveling, he serves as the executive director and founder of The National GUITAR Museum.

Read more about him at newquistbooks.com.

PHOTO CREDITS